Active Denial Memoir: Random Thoughts on Targeting

By Stephen P. Watson

ISBN: 9798630053237

About The Author

My name is Stephen P. Watson, l graduated from college majoring in Liberal Arts. My hobby is music and I have researched many subject matters. I believe in autonomy and open source Information. This may upset the government who believes in controlling people and lots of secrecy/ special interest. I consider myself an Earthling part of the human race where rights should be respected.

Government by Nature is Deceptive

The government increasingly uses euphemisms to mask abuses like changing the Havana Syndrome to anomalous health effects that has a vague meaning intended to no imply anything directly since the government has a motivation to mature directed energy weapons and it changed non lethal weapons to intermediate force. Non-lethal weapons have been tied to abuse by the authorities where there are some lawyers who specialize in taser abuse cases involving law enforcement. A taser would be considered a conducted energy device (CED). Torture is extraordinary rendition. Of course the government or military will not admit in torture so a new name had to be invented describing a procedure like interrogation. Intelligence contractors that work for the government use weasel wording on their web sites describing their services that amounts to a targeting people industry, many claiming to mitigate against threats. Potential whistle blowers like an Edward Snowden are called insider threats. Insider threats sound bad but whistle blowing can actually be good especially in the case of government waste and government corruption. The FBI too is in on the wordplay action using terms like lone offenders, domestic extremist, and conspiracy theory driven domestic extremist, plus many more names for potential threats. There's no name for the Washington D.C. political conspiracy involving TikTok. It's starts with TikTok and before you know it the Chinese have taken over. What about online dating scams? You know people from Taiwan and the Philippines mascaraing as attractive Asians convincing us of Crypto schemes? The Chinese are now controlling our hearts and are minds. When is the last time you feared a conspiracy theory driven domestic extremist and needed help from the FBI to protect you from the conspiracy believers? I think Qanon was a passing fad or are there still believers that the public should be worried about. Thankfully society got through those who believed in the Trillateral Commission. What about the scary white man? The FBI calls those white supremacy extremist and they are a threat to the electric grid. It's like they make this stuff up playing scrabble with nothing to do since there seems to be a lack of real terrorist or super villains. You shouldn't question the government even if they have a poor track record of telling the truth or inventing BS terms called euphemisms. Questioning the government will make you anti-government and the FBI has a break down of different anti-American groups, you know those that believe in false flags? The Truthers, those who used to protest at the site of the 9-11 attacks believing it to be conspiracy have seemed to have gone away though so the Truther movement is something you don't have to worry about. The antivaxxer movement is still fresh in people's minds, not so much the one million plus coronavirus deaths where there's no 9-11 Memorial. It would take a long time to read off those names. Could you imagine, a million names. Maybe convert one of America's abandon shopping malls as a giant memorial. Don't get me started on Active Shooter conspiracies. Targeted Individuals have already gone down that rood with Aaron Alexis and Myron May amongst others. I guess that makes them super-conspiratorial. Driving people to become active shooters for gun control legislation has to be a new government low if true. I was targeted (I was against the UFO cover-up) over UFOs and boy did the government give that an honest take. If you can make sense out of the governments spectacle over UAP, another one of those name changes because UFO is not serious enough, then you are some type of genius that can actually interpret Kama Harris word salad ramblings. The bottom line by nature Government is not very truthful to the people and people by nature are distrustful of the government. This could be why there is a lack of public interest in the government's inquiry about UFOs, like it's just political posturing used as a distraction. The government seems more about alarmism due to failed policy both foreign and domestic. Not only is the country in decline but it's become more corrupt affecting people's bottom line. For this reason, I will not give the government's efforts to investigate UFOs (what it terms UAP) much attention. There is another reason: the government has not revealed much to the public. The only thing you can get out of the government's stance on UFOs is that it represents a threat, like with everything else these days because the sky is falling. Today's UFO threat may have to do with geo-political timing because of the rise of other countries that have fully embraced modernization of their military and economy but again not much has been revealed about the actual UFO subject matter but more so implied. An analogy could be made to the government's concerns over Iraq following 9-11-01. It turns out these concerns were unfounded, even deceptive but that didn't stop our government from hysterics over Iraq. Alarmism and threats justify more spending, more programs etc. It was true then and it is true now. Instead this book will be more educational where the public will get more out of it based on my own research from sources that can be seen by all, also called open-source information. It's the exact opposite of the government's reliance on secrecy and wasting lots of money where the public gets little from it. There will also be no new euphemisms or acronyms to replace old words of the same meaning - a ploy used by the deceptive government. I've written to my elected political representatives, senator Alex Padilla who's a member of the Judiciary and Homeland Security Government Affairs committee and the targeting became stronger. Alex Padilla looks like a used car salesman with slicked back hair, unpopular VP Kamal Harris was his predecessor. He's involved in Homeland Security and expressed concern about homegrown extremism within the Federal agency. I'm sure that's on everybody's mind, a future Capital rioter like on January Six could be a TSA screener or one of those DHS people who sit around doing nothing. Case in point the border. I also wrote the California Governor Gavin Newsom who is one of the technology 'innovation' worshippers criticized as being out of touch in California's decline. He's like a wannabe Lex Luther, maybe too busy admiring himself while staring in the mirror. There was no response from Senator Dianne Feinstein who previously looked into Gitmo torture with the Senate Intelligence Committee report on CIA torture while she still had her faculties. The torture report was something the CIA wanted to desperately sweep under the rug. Dianne Feinstein is now deceased and was in a vegetable state while still serving when I contacted her. If there was a good argument for term limits it would be Dianne Feinstein who looked like something off Tales Form The Crypt. It looks like she will be replaced by Adam Schiff, another alarmist who has an unhealthy obsession with Trump, part of past government disfunction. Other politicians I contacted were Senator Chuck Schumer and Charles Rangel when I lived in New York. Senator Chuck Schumer seemed very fond of the 9-11 anniversary not missing a chance to make an appearance at the 9-11 memorial each year. Some 9-11 victims families even complained of how it was being politicized saying enough, just stop already. He gave the commencement speech when I graduated from BMCC college while I received a directed energy attack. It was to the neck to try and cause paroxysmal (forced) coughing while Schumer was staring directly at me like an Emperor Palpatine from Star Wars using the dark side. Schumer mostly ranted about Trump and stated that he (Schumer) was only good at politics where he found his calling while attending an ivy league school. I.e. a career politician. Some people have gotten themselves in trouble by threatening politicians so you have to me matter-of-fact and polite when writing to them even though they are slime balls and are spineless. Most politicians are afraid of January Six or an angry mob with pitch forks and torches, a tactic used in the past to expunge political vermin, although it would be unwise unless staging a coup d'etat was successful and that usually happens in the developing world in the form of a military coup. In college I was taught that writing a politician does no good. Another reason politicians ignore individual concerns is there is a lack of incentive to act because of who may be involved. It represents a type of pandoras box. They'd rather turn a blind eye to abuse like electronic harassment and go along with a wild goose chase holding congressional hearings over UFOs or jus be alarmist for the sake of alarmism.

The Rise of Government UAP Alarmism During The 2000s

I remember a year after the US Nimitz encounter allegedly occurred there was a UFO invasion TV show called Threshold where the first episode depicted a strange UFO encounter by a Navy ship. The UFO depicted was not a flying saucer or a traditional UFO but some computer generated morphing object made of light. Threshold the TV series did not last and neither did another TV series from the same time named Invasion, a it was like a take on Invasion of the Body Snatchers that aired on network TV and so did Surface about the threat from the sea - a sea monster. Were these TV shows just a coincidence? Probably not. It aired right after Peter Jeening had a UFO special entitled Seeing Is Believing. The public at that time was not interested or very frightened by UFOs - probably watching internet porn on their computers. The Pentagon's AAWSAP (Advanced

Aerospace Weapon Systems Application Program) and Advanced Threat Identification Program (AATIP) says it all. UFOs are just another threat to play up and it has to involve the DARPA dogs. i.e. weapon systems. The US Government playing up UFO alarmism has another problem: WMD's in Iraq. I.e. the public has been lied to before like the boy who cried wolf so naturally people embrace UFO 'false flag' conspiracies like a Project Blue Beam. There's also the elephant in the room that can't be acknowledged - the black budget, so the right hand doesn't know what the left hand is doing. Alarmism became more of a political tactic after 9-11. It's like the reverse of the McCarthyism days; instead of the threat of communism it's like the sky is falling, everything is a threat - in this case UFOs that were spotted by Navy pilots, or were they? The video can't be disputed or can it? Video analysis Mick West makes a compelling argument of how the so called Navy UFO encounter videos are just camera artifacts, birds, and possibly an airplane at a distance. The so called Gimbal UFO for example is just the jet's own exhaust reflected on the jet's Raytheon IR camera. The actual UFO would not be observed by the pilot because it was too far away and the pilot is getting excited about what he sees on the radar screen. Another video is explained as a bird that's actually not moving very fast - it's an optical illusion because the jet is going fast the other direction. There's the real possibility there was no UFO - alas, fooled by an over-reliance on technology. Is anyone surprised? Like the door falling off a Boeing-built jumbo jet plane mid flight. There's no technology substitution for competence or human error. The Navy probably saw all the commotion was not over a UFO and decided to just stay quiet and taking note of false pilots perceptions due to the equipment for future adjustments. People get promoted over being well liked versus having any real skills. The fighter jet pilots were probably fighter aces because of good looks like Tom Cruise on Top Gun but not the Red Baron when it comes to flying a plane. The Navy is probably just thankful they can land a plane on a ship without crashing it. Most soldiers will never see any real combat and dropping bombs on targets does not count. Technology had duped us all and often appears overly-complex. Most are too lazy to read the instruction manual to a new technology device, I'm sure the geniuses at the US armed forces are no exception. How does this Raytheon IR camera actually work? One thing telling about the Pentagon's leaked footage is other countries including are allies did not see the same "tic-tac" object that is depicted as a flying propane tank. Another telling thing is the lack of independent video confirmation - that's not an IR dark blob image but actual video of the craft. I also speculate after the declassified UFOs got media attention there was some embellishment to make the UFO threat seem real to politicize the subject matter.

My Electronic Harassment Begins From Posting To UFO Forums During the Early 2000s

My Dad who had an interest in flying saucers was a bit of a maverick but was not involved in aerospace. He had employment problems in America, getting fired from Texas Instruments and Xerox, eventually moving back to Italy and retiring as a welder. After re-connecting with him in 2013 he explained more about what he was trying to do building a flying saucer and his discovery of electric wind using a van Der Graff. I was young at the time and only recalled him trying to build the frame of a flying saucer but never completing it. My targeting began not from my Dad's attempts at building a flying saucer but from posting to the internet starting in the early 2000s. Pretty much at the time I was a slacker that trolled the internet. I moved from Stephenville, Texas to Dallas in the year 2000 had bad acne, no friends, I was a loner. The FBI had the term 'loner offender' and I'm sure I fit the psychological profile. My trolling the internet, posting to UFO forums, and compiling my own research put me on the government's radar like some geek who didn't get out much and spent too much time on the computer. I remember back in the early 2000s I rented an apartment at 7373 Valley View Lane not far away from Texas Instruments. At home I had a Macintosh 7500 computer with a 33.6K dial up modem and a landline phone. During my downtime I would post to music mailing list and UFO forums becoming somewhat of an arm chair researcher. My interest in UFOs started after hearing Art Bell on the radio while working overnight as a security guard. Unbeknownst to me The Pentagon was alarmed over UFOs, this could have been before the Advanced Threat Identification Program (ATIP) costing tax payers 22 million dollars, partly due to eccentric Billionaire Robert Bigelow approaching Harry Reid to look into the UFO subject matter. I remember the year was 2003 or 2004. Around that time I started to become electronic harassed. I was being hit with a crude form of directed energy (DE) and knew it was not something normal. After getting into a debate, or flame wars, with a UFO debunkers on UFO forums I would get this high-pitched tone that would come into my left ear, the type of tone in a hearing test, and then fade out followed by a sinus migraine and mild TBI symptoms where my head felt numb like a brick. I had trouble concentrating, and had slurred speech. The electronic harassment only reinforced my belief that I was onto something, it made me mad, so I continued to look into UFOs. I noticed commonalities in UFO reports and created a web site on Geocities where I could hyperlink HTML (web) pages and cross reference the UFO commonalities I was seeing. For example there were many flying saucer reports but also reports of saucer craft that were silvery-metallic in appearance with no seams or riveting. Also many reports of UFO's glowing at night like the craft was ionizing the air, creating plasma. I started creating more and more web pages noticing more

UFO commonalities and also going to UFO forums. At work a new security guard who served in Iraq sat beside me at an employee meeting and out of the blue brought up the topic of UFOs, even turning to me and asking about them. I thought it was odd, thinking he may have been trying to embarrass me like he knew that I posted about UFOs to the internet debating UFO debunkers, like he was some type of informant. The guard who served in Iraq worked there for a short time and then left. I continued to research UFOs while working as a security guard and my research never went into hacking, only HTML pages that I would hyperlink and cross reference, I was never a coding nerd. I never had a high level of technical expertise or access to classified material. I wasn't Gary McKinnon, the British UFO hacker that claimed to see information regarding space fleets or a picture of a cigar-shaped UFO in space, or that building 8 at Johnson Space Center (JSC Building 8) was airbrushing out images of UFOs.

Delusions of Grandeur and UFOs

Like others in government who want to grab the UAP spotlight I was suffering from delusions of UFO grandeur. I thought UFO technology being covered-up was a break through, enamored with innovation, and thoughts I could change the course of human history by exposing the conspiracy after hearing Art Bell (radio). This is also what Harry Reid thought in funding the Advance Aerospace Threat Identification Program (AATIP). UFO technology breakthroughs would give the USA the lead for time to come thanks to the urging of Robert Bigelow - like sticking a carrot in front of a donkey and making it walk forward. It did not turn out that way because Bigelow's efforts turned out to be a lot of quackery, partly due to the cast of experts he relied on. Part of the problem of being rich is you're often told what you want to hear by those eager to please. I could see where Robert Bigelow was coming from looking beyond conventional science exploring far-fetched exotic technology concepts and even the paranormal but bending spoons using your mind will not land humans on Mars. My Favorite Martian was just a TV show and should not be taken seriously. Looking at the acronyms of the programs that were funded I can't help but suspect there may have been more to the funding. With AAWSAP/AATIP there's emphasis on the words weapons and threats. My electronic harassment coincided with posting to UFO forums. The wording of course could have also had to do with funding approval since its hard to justify millions if it was worded Bigelow's UFO wild goose chase obsession. From my research Robert Bigelow was convinced UFOs were real after seeing a flying saucer himself and that it was a source of technology breakthroughs and aggressively pursued UFO evidence using his wealth paying alien abduction researchers when alien abductions was popular because of the X-Files; funding the UFO organization MUFON to gain access to UFO cases that had non-disclosure agreements, and funded a team at MUFON for boots-on-the-ground investigations of some of the more intriguing cases. He used Neo-liberal tactics like trying to use government funding for AATIP and received airline pilot reports from then FAA; he purchased a ranch with reported supernatural and UFO activity. Bigelow was convinced that the Universe was comprised of haves and have-nots. Yes, it's a cold dog eat dog world out there too. Some civilizations were highly advanced while others like Earth were not there yet, if ever. Like there's an Alpha Centauri Dubai where the cocktail lounge is just for those who discovered advanced space faring technology with a flying saucer VIP parking lot attracting interstellar capitalist who are part of an elite club. Those UFOs, they are not from around here, it's like the UFOs don't obey the laws of physics, have the control of gravity, can zip off to light speed. It almost sounds too good to be true, after all look at the advancements we made in the modern era, surely what appears impossible to known science can be achieved knowing nothing about aviation, sciences and physics - forget about logical fallacies or deductive reasoning, just pay so-called experts like Bigelow does since he has the money for what seems like a trivial pursuit. Robert Bigelow made his money in real estate investments or hotel chains. From interviews Robert Bigelow describes seeing a UFO and that inspired to delve into the subject matter. He conceded the only way he can achieve that level of advancement is by becoming rich - like a mule chasing a cart on a stick but never being able to get it. After becoming wealthy Bigelow surrounded himself with people that could be considered quacks or promoted pseudo-science. That's partly due to the nature of the subject matter - it delves into the unknowns, mysteries. This is also the case with Tom DeLonge and his To The Stars Academy that was intended to be a benefit corporation using alien-tech to help the US military and the world. People who received a high degree and success think the trajectory is always upward (no pun UFOs) but the earth always has a tendency to make people who think to highly of themselves to come crashing back down. Crowd funding didn't pan out and nor some breakthrough because of UFO evidence and To The Stars Academy had to reduce its ambitions to entertainment according to an SEC filing. Defense-intel people associated with To The Stars parted ways. Meanwhile Robert Bigelow's warehouse in Las Vegas full of UFO debris hoarding could not save Bigelow Aerospace. You think a guy that paid people for UFO exclusives and cozied up tho the Area 51 government could build a spaceship but this is not the case. The VIP section at the Alpha Centauri cocktail lounge had to cancel Bigelow's reservation - he could not make it or even get to space. So much for the Neo-liberal space industry - maybe in another 50 years. Fast forward to today and Bigelow could not fulfill Harry Reid's hopes of UFOs putting America way ahead of the competition because real science is not pseudo-science. A car does not run on fairy dust nor does aircraft on anti-gravity. Until someone could prove alien UFO hardware is not modern lore than a person, even a billionaire may just be spinning their wheels. The millions spent on AATIP only served Robert Bigelow's UFO evidence hoarding and curiosity. Bigelow is much older and like Harry Reid looking at the grim reaper so Bigelow has an essay contest to convince him of life after death paying the winner a million dollars but try getting everything you want when your dead - money is meaningless - the devil will just laugh at you showing the contract where you sold your soul in order to be successful. Most affluent people probably didn't achieve a high degree of wealth the honest way did nor politicians climbing to power. The moral of the story? Sometimes people get too full of themselves after achieving success and have delusions of grandeur. No matter how much wealth and fame you have you're still not God. A reader may think I'm bashing Robert Bigelow and Tom DeLonge but I'm not - just illustrating 'delusions of grandeur.' Sure there is the slim chance you could defy scientific rigor and discover a magic carpet or a time travel machine where fantasy becomes reality but it generally doesn't happen. There's probably no portals at Skinwalker Ranch either. My grandfather had some farmland with cows. Nothing unusual going on there, only the smell of manure. My father, Gene Watson (not the country singer) wanted to build a flying saucer in the

backyard of a rental house even to the point of angering
local city officials and economic hardship. He used to tell
me as a kid that he was going to build a flying saucer and
it was going to make us rich while he drove me to school
and that he would land in front of the school and drop me
off, how does that sound? While chuckling. My dad was a
smart person and could have become an electrician,
engineer, or scientist but was preoccupied in what others
would see as trivial pursuits like building a saucer. He
relied of dumpster diving at industrial parks for scrap
metal and electronics, also picking up beer cans with me
tagging along because he was always broke and my
maternal grandparents would always have to help out on
rent. While welding a flying saucer together he would
always change his mind not getting past building a metal
frame where he was going to put a car engine inside. My
big sister made him mad by calling him a dreamer and my
dad didn't see himself as a dreamer but compared himself
to the Wright Brothers. As our family grew toward the
end of the 1980s things became tougher, he was reduced
to delivering pizza's and had a religious side. He started
to exhibit bizarre behavior building a Virgin Mary shrine
in the woods and write long religious diatribe letters. My
mother had enough and filed for divorce, he blamed my
grandfather for his troubles and my Mom's evangelical
church where he got on a plane and bailed to Italy. His
Italian relatives urged him to go back but he refused
eventually helping him get a job as a welder where the
dream of building a flying saucer faded and even his love

for the Catholic Church where he just believed in God. My Dad however continued electrical experiments making ion lifters but knew the dream of building a saucer was behind him, not resulting in fame or prosperity. It affected his view of people, that any good idea will just be ripped off by wealthy industrialist and greedy corporations and even the patent office is rigged so the government can steal inventions. Fast forward 20 years later and I had delusions of grandeur believing in the same modern philosophy enamored by technological breakthroughs and innovation. After hearing about a UFO cover-up on the overnight paranormal talk radio show Art Bell, I believed I could be an armchair UFO researcher looking into conspiracies and UFO cases exposing the UFO cover-up. Think how the world would change if it were known the government was hiding crashed alien saucers at Hanger 18. In a short amount of time the human race could be flying in spaceships amongst the planets in our solar system like depicted in science fiction. While debating UFO debunkers on UFO forums during the dial-up internet days of the early 2000s I started to receive electronic harassment. It only served as validation that I was onto something. I felt I was getting closer to the truth but in the years to come my armchair internet research efforts never resulted in disclosure. Instead a decade later the term UFO changed to UAP and became more alarmism for the government. Old Ufologist died off and there was a new cast of characters spouting the same anti-gravity, warping time and space nonsense.

The Murky Pseudo-Science History of UAP

AAWSAP/AATIP was a UFO research program by the
Pentagon, partly due to Robert Bigelow convincing then
Senator Harry Reid to look into the matter, the
AAWSAP/AATIP program was from the years 2007-
2012 and was not revealed to the public at the time,
although the Pentagon's interest in UFOs could have been
much earlier. Most people know it as the Advanced
Aerospace Threat Identification (AATIP) program.
AAWSAP (Advanced Aerospace Weapon Systems
Application Program) was another program by the DIA
that overlapped with AATIP. It looked at advanced and
theoretical concepts that may hold the key to potential
scientific breakthroughs like in reported in UFO
sightings. Skinwalker Ranch was also involved in the
program and there was speculation that Skinwalker Ranch
was really a testing ground for weapons that dealt with
UFO technology instead of bizarre paranormal activity as
the name AAWSAP (Advanced Aerospace Weapon
Systems Application Program) implies. Why would it use
the word "weapons" if it was just looking at pseudo-
science concepts like transversal wormholes? There was
some speculation that the weapons part could be an
explanation to the Navy UFOs. Someone messing with
the radar and even creating false images using plasma

decoys using lasers. The Navy was a test-bed to see if the USA's modern jets can be fooled by these false UFO images and decoys that look real on the jets radar. My harassment coincidentally occurred when I was posting to UFO forums followed by getting electronic harassed including MUFON's Internet forum when Bigelow was funding the Star Team (boots on the ground investigators funded by Bigelow). Robert Bigelow who can be viewed as an eccentric, non apologetic about his belief in aliens, and an opportunist hoarding UFO evidence in a Las Vegas Warehouse is said to be the sole contractor that received AAWSAP funding for experiments through his BAASS organization that also received FAA pilot reports of UFOs. Bigelow started numerous organizations in the past like the now defunct National Institute of Discovery Science (NIDS), that was considered a pseudo-scientific organization, some names associated with NIDS were part of the "invisible college" into remote viewing and psychic phenomenon. Bigelow would use his wealth to buy what he saw as compelling evidence from researchers. One such story involved an alien abduction hypnotherapist named John Carpenter part of MUFON's Alien Abduction Transcription Project during a time in the 1990s when alien abduction was popular because of the X-Files TV Show. Carpenter allegedly sold Robert Bigelow his alien abduction research including names of the abductees. The use of hypnosis to acquire accurate information is controversial due to a person using their imagination like from seeing the X-Files or the hypnotherapist being suggestive. Skeptics have accused Robert Bigelow of surrounding himself with charlatans and pseudo scientist and what was being researched according to documentation on AATIP amounted nothing more than science fiction or was it? Maybe stealth weapons? When the program ended some within AATIP blamed a secret cabal at the Pentagon who were not in favor of UFO research because aliens could be demon manifestations, this belief was due to their own religious convictions. Remember the Access of Evil was called clash of civilizations. Judeo-Christian Neo-Cons against The Islamic Fundamentalist who called American's infidels. AATIP made news in 2017 long after the program was canceled, also the War in Iraq and Afghanistan didn't turn out to be a clash of civilizations but a prolonged land occupation. America did not win over the hearts and minds of people in Iraq or Afghanistan, they still embraced their old values and beliefs. News of AATIP came after the leaking of the US Nimitz 'tic-tac' UFO that can be viewed as a publicity stunt (involving a former disgruntled AATIP employee) to help promoted a new private venture with some of the same Bigeow people called 'To The Stars Academy.' To The Stars Academy, that initially got off the ground (no pun) using an umbrella company or angel investor, where a former CIA officer was listed as co-founder, it was going to be crowd funded - a benefit corporation, the front man was a rock singer who was supposed to make the company cool to the masses, it even signed a contract with the Army to look at alleged alien material from UFO crashes or alleged alien implants (maybe from Bigelow's warehouse?). To The Stars Academy fell short. There was a lack of enthusiasm, or more importantly crowd funding, and the defense-intelligence spooks who had prestigious roles at To The Stars Academy parted ways leaving the rocker focusing on entertainment. The leaked Pentagon UAP footage spurred congressional interest in UFOs even though there was not that much demand or interest by the public. It's one thing to have a popular science fiction show like Stranger Things but another thing to have the public to become serious about UFOs observed by the Nazy, especially when leaked video looks like a dark blob or a zoom-in of a horse fly buzzing around the camera. Most of the politicians that demanded answers over UAP were naive and didn't know much about UFOs. Politicians like Marco Rubio (R-Florida) and Kristen Gillibrand (D-N.Y.) (who's lives must be very boring) demand to know answers. In 2020 under President Trump using a COVID-19 relief bill there was an order for US Intelligence (IC) to deliver a UAP report to congress (Congressional Intelligence Committees). People in UFOlogy claimed the report was very elementary and short like written by a college student and really didn't say much. In 2021 there was the creation of the UAP Task force (UAPTF) that turned into the acronym AOIMSG and then in 2022 under the National Defense Authorization Act the name was changed to 'AARO' tasked with investigating UFOs where the Department of

Justice (DoJ) is listed as one of the key partners and stakeholders. AARO is also linked with the DIA, DoD, and other Federal Agencies tasked with 'mitigating' threats associated with UAP. An news article from 2021 says the FBI investigated a flying humanoid on a jetpack that occurred around Los Angeles and an article from 2023 claimed the FBI tasked with investigating UAP visited the Falcon Space Lab using a Geiger counter to test for radiation because of an anonymous tip. The lab was looking into UFO propulsion testing various theories. It was bootstrapped by a community of scientist, engineers, inventors etc. and funded by donations and private investors. The Falcon Space Lab denied any harmful radiation was being used. One of the men associated with AATIP and later the UAP Task Force named Jay Stratton left his role at the Pentagon in 2021 to work for a defense-intelligence contractor named Radiance Technologies where directed energy (DE) is listed on its web site as once of their specialties. As pointed out earlier the DoJ's research arm the National Institute of Justice along with Raytheon were working on Assault Intervention Device (AID) with a desire to make it more portable, sold-state, and put in the hand of law enforcement. The Pentagon has documentation on directed energy intermediate force capabilities (DE IFC) with a range of non lethal weapon directed energy (DE & NLW) devices. I observed after compiling UFO commonalities and then researching targeted individuals (TI's) there were some similarities. For example DEWs and lots of UFO beam reports. Telepathic communication by UFO occupants and V2K. Alien implants and Technology-Based Tagging, Tracking, and Locating. David Grusch UFO whistleblower claims recovered crashed UFOs were reverse engineered to make weapons could be spreading disinformation but I knew my electronic harassment coincided with my UFO research and posting to UFO forums at the time of the AAWSAP (Advanced Aerospace Weapon Systems Application Program). In 2022 it was reported that Luis Elizondo former director of AATIP became a contractor for the Space Force (USSF).

Recovered UFO Craft Reverse Engineered and Used As Weapons According To Insider

Robert Bigelow who was obsessed with UFOs was very concerned about China and its growing interest in the subject matter. It is said China now uses AI to keep track of many of its UFO sightings and does not believe they are piloted by little green men. The Pentagon's UAP program was later canceled but still existed in some facet until the newly, more recent created UAP government bureaucracy (AARO) and I'm sure this was also the case with the non-lethal directed energy weapons (NLW DE) or projecting voices into people's skulls using microwaves (the Frey effect) like with V2K, those type of programs continued. I know this because of my own DE targeting. Interestingly enough, before AATIP, the Pentagon's UAP program was called the AAWSAP (Advanced Aerospace Weapon Systems Application Program) and there may have been more to the program that dealt with weapons. The name Skinwalker Ranch reminds me of Raytheon Ranch where Raytheon weaponry like directed energy weapons are tested. Yuma Proving Ground in Utah where weapons are tested is sometimes referred to as Area 52. Skinwalker Ranch according to reports is also located in Utah. In the 2000s there was controversy with Raytheon Missile Systems testing weapons at a ranch near Cochise County north of Wilcox, Arizona. Raytheon's deputy director claimed the cost are a fraction of what it cost to test weapons at military bases. This Neo-liberal approach could give a clue why Skinwalker Ranch would have appeal in secretly testing weapons relating to UFOs. During the early 2000s Active Denial, the non-lethal counter-personnel weapon was tested at Kirkland Air Force Base, south of Albuquerque, New Mexico and then in 2005 there was Project Sheriff testing it's short-ranged non-lethal millimeter wave weapon for urban warfare placed on the back of a Stryker vehicle that was tested at the Naval Surface Warfare center, in Dahlgren, Virginia; Quantico, Virgina (same city as FBI training); and Yuma Proving Grounds, Arizona. In more recent news in 2023 it was reported that Raytheon partnered with Texas A&M to test a HEL (a high energy laser) on the Texas A&M

RELLIS at the George H.W. Bush Combat Development Complex (BCDC) campus. Raytheon has a laser weapon factory in McKinney, Texas and White Sands Missile range serves as a test bed for its laser weapons, this laser weapon wa pallet sized and could be hauled on the back of a truck designed to shoot (zap) down down drones that it terms asymmetrical warfare threats. The term "acquire, track, target and destroy" is used. It can be used to target stand-alone or warms of drones and operated by a laptop and a video game-style controller also plugged into a long list of of air defense or command and control systems. This is important because when driving around in LA I get the impression I'm tracked and my targeting is controlled from somewhere. I can only speculate if it's from a police station or command center used by a contractor. Laser weapons aren't exactly a new concept, they've come along because of solid state (SS DE) technology. When I was researching UFOs and compiling UFO reports were many reports of UFO projecting beams or telepathic communication by alien beings. The story's coming out of Robert Bigelow's Skinwalker Ranch in Utah like portal openings, poltergeist activity, monsters seemed too fantastic to be true. A so called UFO whistle blower named David Grusch testifying before the House Oversight Committee national security subcommittee claimed that the US was using crashed alien UFO's to develop weapons. David Grusch whether legit or not (it has since been revealed he has a history of mental health issues) seemed to echo Philip Corso from decades earlier who wrote the book The Day After Roswell asserting UFO crash cover-ups and reverse engineering. There were USAF UFO crash recovery crews that did bring material to Write Patterson AFB under Project Moon Dust and Blue Fly. Skeptics claim such programs were really recovering foreign technology like a downed spy satellite. A MIG-21 fighter plane was recovered intact and flown at Area 51 during the Cold War in 1968.

The Move To New York City in 2006

The earliest form of my electronic harassment occurred in Texas living in Richardson, Texas and commuting to a security guard job at DFW airport that would eventually end in the summer of 2006 with no more work and I fell on hard times. I was not able to secure shelter or receive much help from relatives, my grandparents living in Comanche, Texas said they were too old, and the few friends I had from the 1990s had distanced themselves from me for socio-economic reasons, so I decided to make the move to New York City out of desperation. When I first arrived in New York, I noticed beeping every three seconds on my prepaid phone when placing a call. After a three-month stint of becoming homeless I got back on my feet by becoming a licensed New York security guard and found a room using a room rental agency in East New York. I remember the room rental agency located in Manhattan that I found in the back of the classifieds asked if I was sure I wanted to move to East New York and they re-assured me that if I didn't like the place I could always come back for another room at no charge. So, knowing little about New York City I accepted the offer and went to check out the place. I took the C subway train to Rockaway Avenue where I discovered East New York is mostly African American near the projects. For those who don't know East New York is actually a part of Brooklyn, New York. During the1980s it was considered a very dangerous neighborhood after white flight during the 1960s with the building of the projects. Today, like all things it's more gentrified. When I arrived in late 2006 the neighborhood was still a little rough but was safe enough to walk around during the day. It helped that I dressed down and looked poor. I believe the first address I tried to call I received no answer so I went to see the next apartment on the list which was a brownstone building. A Jamaican lady opened the door and I was able to secure the room with a payment. I lived there for two or three years continuing with my UFO research working as a security guard going from one security guard company to another. I would use a free Wi-Fi connection at the Public Library for my MacBook. Sometimes the crude electronic harassment with the high-pitched tone that would fade in and out of the left ear would occur like when I lived in Texas. After wearing out my welcome with the land lady who was a slumlord in East New York, I decided to move to a new location - a room rental in Hamilton Heights, Upper Manhattan. I purchased a beat-up van from a local rental car business in Brooklyn, standing behind the counter was an Orthodox Jew who said he only had a van to rent with a wobbly tire. I drover carefully hoping the tire would not fall off and made my way to Manhattan. What did not help my electronic harassment situation is I started working with a private security company who's client was a government-connected agency - The Port Authority of New York and New Jersey. In 2012 the PANYNJ centralizing its security and police operations using a private firm of former Homeland Security-Washington DC insiders called The Chertoff Group that included former CIA director Michael Hayden who was accused of misleading Congress on the role of the CIA's torture program. A TI from a 2015 targeted individual protest in Washington named Tyrone Dew even confronted Hayden asking him about DEWs used against civilians. It's a bit coincidental that the more extreme pain ray torture started shortly after The Chertoff Group's involvement. The Chertoff Group had a white paper on the company's web site about "insider threats" as well as being designated for the DHS SAFETY Act that was enacted by Congress in 2002 providing legal liability protection for contractors involved in anti-terror technology.

The Warning Signs at Work; Work Place Mobbing

It seemed someone wasn't too happy with my UFO research obsession. If you recall I received a crude form of electronic harassment before moving to New York which continued after moving to New York. I'm guessing it was someone in government, possibly related to the Pentagons UFO Threat (AATIP) assessment program. My laptop was always out at work during the overnight shift and there was constant CCTV monitoring. Sometimes I would piggyback an unsecured Wi-Fi connection from the restaurant next door. I'm sure this raised suspicion considering I faced intimidation from overnight inspectors at work. More than likely though, the government-related agency I was stationed at was probably alerted by those responsible for the harassment. One inspector was a veteran who was a former Special Operations soldier in Iraq. He suffered from PTSD and had a reputation of being a jerk or bully. He claimed that America does bad stuff to people who threaten national security and was unapologetic when we were talking. It's clear his standard of ethics were purely from a soldier in a battlefield perspective. I believe he got suspended over an incident where a security guard got beat up by an angry pedestrian and the Special Operations vet just stood by and watched. One thing I remember him saying though, and to his credit, that he did not agree with the government dictating free speech, "you can't say this, you can't say that, you can't have supersized soft drinks."

Later there was an inspector who was a former police officer who worked for the Government-Related client. My private security guard employer hires a lot of former cops. He would come by and give me hints that my UFO research was upsetting the government. He would bring up UFOs and get into the subject of the FBI and that they have all these hidden spy devices. I believe he was also involved in a lawsuit over a lack of promotion to sergeant with the government related client. What's interesting is I looked into lawsuits against the government-related client and one woman sued for a peep cam that was installed during a workers comp physical. The government-related client had their own medical facility. I read a court case where a man suing won a million dollars because the cops were trying to spike the amount of arrest by claiming perverted acts were occurring in a train station public restroom.

Intimidation, Warning Sign from Spooks

Right before my mother was targeted and the pain ray assaults began during that time I used to go to the Mid-Manhattan Library near Bryant Park on 40th street and 5th avenue because of their DVD movie selection. I used to go there for the old Doctor Who episodes and foreign films as well as the free Wi-Fi. In fact, remember at the time the Public Library was my number one source or

Wi-Fi using a MacBook. I remember after posting to a UFO forum or compiling UFO info I went downstairs to the DVD section and a man who seemed out of place wearing black camo, tactical clothing started walking in my area repeating "mommy, mommy." He has the appearance of a defense contractor. He came across as not being from the area. His camo looking clothing appeared too clean, like it was just purchased. I just brushed the encounter off. This person would appear again when I was looking at DVDs wearing the same clothes. This time I caught the stranger off guard by turning around real quick and walking his direction right after I felt the high pitch tone fading in and out of my left ear, he appeared to panic and quickly put a hand held device in his pocket. I was tempted to reach in his pocket and grab the hand-held device and run off but didn't. Another strange event occurred that I can't really explain since I was pretty much a loner is I received a strange text message in while staying in my rental room. I posted to a forum about shooting at UFOs to see if the craft are top secret or piloted by aliens when it crashes. Then later when I was home I received a text message that read "I can shoot you right now if I want to."

2013 The Pain Ray 'Active Denial' Abuse began. Monrovia, California & Hamilton Heights

I started to receive the pain ray, more extreme and constant electronic harassment in the Spring of 2013. It was not only me but my mother who was renting a room in a two-story house located in Monrovia, California. It coincided with some rather suspect activity of a person dragging equipment on the floor above me and feeling directed energy or unbearable pain to my head and stomach. At the time I had been renting a room in a five or six story building located in Hamilton Heights after moving from East New York. My mother would report the same activity. She was located on the bottom floor and thought equipment being used to harass was from mischievous people above her. She would try calling the Monrovia police to no avail, they would do nothing and my big sister who also lives in California would eventually move her to a retirement home unwilling to believe that such a thing could be occurring. Meanwhile as I was getting assaulted by the pain ray in my room rental it was also happening at work, as I worked overnight and was posted in the lobby. It seemed to be coming from the ceiling above me as if there was equipment concealed and would dissipate if I left the area. The strange thing is one of the ceiling light fixtures directly above would always go out with the light needing to be replaced. It seemed the main purpose of this pain ray weapon abuse was to cause sleep deprivation since the targeting was heavy at home when I would lie down on the bed to go to sleep. My mother would also claim the same thing, especially when being targeted in the two-story house in Monrovia. She described the perpetrators as young men on the floor above and described the sensation of feeling waves moving across the body. She also described a phenomenon other TI's being electronic harassed describe and that is what is termed sexual-touching. It's when the electronic harassment can be felt in the private areas. I don't experience this often but sometimes it does occur like being targeted in the anal region. There was also what she describes as flashes of light. This may have been due to her having a metal plate in her head because of experimental brain surgery she had to have during the early 1970s due to black outs and seizures. I payed a visit to the house some years later during a trip to California. It was a wooden two-story house and appeared to be a boarding house with a number of tenants judging from the front porch area that had signage and mailboxes. I proceeded to take some photographs. The landlord or person who oversaw the place appeared to be not at home. I also payed a visit to the Monrovia Police Department inquiring about police records and was given a form to list the date and time of the alleged incidents in order to pull up a record. It was unclear if there would be any records since as previously mentioned the police would just show up after she dialed 911 and do nothing and leave. Inaction by law enforcement is commonly reported by targeted individuals. My mother when questioned was less-than cooperative and didn't want to bring up disturbing things of the past or me even going to the house thinking that it would just stir up more trouble.

Spring 2013; 144th Street, Upper Manhattan, Hamilton Heights – The Pain Ray begins

In the summer of 2013 things came to a head in my room rental in Hamilton Heights on 144th street. I had been living there for awhile and was now being hit with the pain ray from the floor above. The tenant I was renting a room from became ill with cancer, She was already taking medication when I first moved in but was now going in and out of the hospital, so I had to move by a certain date. By this time the entire apartment was empty with exception of myself. The pain ray I was being hit with was intense inside my rental room. I remember buying an old army helmet at the military surplus store and going away from the room rental I usually stayed in and sat in the living room where the tenants usually occupied just sitting there deciding my next move with the army helmet over my head. It was temporary relief from the pain ray harassment. I don't recall if I was followed. I think maybe later on, the perpetrator on the floor above noticed I would go outside my room to the living room but it was time to plan my next move. I went back to a room rental agency to find another tenant and would find another room on 147th street. This would have been the late spring or summer of 2013. It was hot and I moved my belongings, music equipment using a pushcart - traveling back and forth to the new room rental.

Spring to Autumn 2013; 544 West 147 Street Apt 3D & Broadway

This was another five or six story building. The room I was renting was on the third floor. The previous building that I rented a room on 144th street had an elevator. This building had only stairs. So it was a real chore to move my stuff going up and down the stairs. In this apartment I was renting the room from a young couple with a small boy - their grandmother would occasionally come by. I mostly saw the woman who I believe went by the name GiGi, at least that is what she wanted me to call her. What I always remember about this building is it had a long hallway with a chandelier leading up to the stairs. The stairs were winding going up to each floor that contained three or four apartment dwellings with room numbers followed by a letter. As I completed my move I felt bad for the older woman I used to rent a room from who fell ill and her family sold the apartment. She was a very nice person. Where I was now renting a room it was a young couple with their first child and I forget if my room was closest to the door, I believe it was, but the move was complete. Interestingly enough though, during the move it seemed the directed energy when it first started out was intense. i had a giant welt on the back of my neck. Now I felt relieved that I had escaped the ugly harassment where equipment could be heard dragging on the floor above me pacing my location. Some days past and I distinctly remember walking up the stairs past two men, one mid-aged and the other and older man wearing a black hat that reminded me of the old 1950 gangster movies or the Men In Black. I got the impression the old man was the leader or handler. The harassment probably was a team effort involving more than one perpetrator. They were both struggling to carry something heavy up the steps in what looked like a box container that was wrapped in a black plastic bag so people could not see the contents inside. I went up up the steps past them acting nonchalant and turned around to look down and have another look after I got aways up. They stopped in their tracks and looked straight up at me with a blank stare - like the equipment was intended for me. I don't think they were anticipating that I would be there in the building during that time and I caught the two men off-guard. As coincidence would have it, shortly afterward the electronic harassment would start up again. As I lied down on the bed feeling a bit tired and stressed I experienced something like voice-to-skull. The sound could be described as one of those beeping tones you hear in a hearing test. I also remember at the time, especially when my pain ray harassment first started there was a strong tinnitus in my left ear. I recall one day I'm my previous room rental feeling groggy like I had been drugged. It makes me wander if I was implanted or tagged. An older private intelligence agency called Blackbird Technologies specialized in what is called Tagging Tracking and Locating (TTL). The technology from my understanding would allow anyone who was tagged to be tracked electronically. It was an interesting theory of how the left ear always got the ringing, but I did not have the equipment or know how in oder to see if I was tagged, anyway I remember shortly after the men were moving concealed equipment up the stairs here came equipment being dragged on the floor above me again pacing my position. This time instead of using an army helmet I wanted to try passive shielding. I knew I was being hit with directed energy but knew little about how to shield from it. So I made my way to the hardware store. I bought lots of wire mesh and stapled it to the ceiling. Then I bought square metal plates; also some plywood. I remember hauling all this material on the subway, into the building, up the stairs into the room hoping to not be noticed. It was also not all at once but over time too. Sometimes it would be material I found on the street - stuff people threw out. Around the time my pain ray electronic harassment started up again I met the perpetrator rather indirectly. As I was walking up the steps to my rental room on the third floor behind me followed an aged 20-something African American male. He was about average height, lean, and somewhat muscular with a shaven bald head. I got to the apartment to open the door, he walked and got right up to my face, similar to boxers staring each other down before a bout. I didn't do or say anything or I may have said something neighborly, or asked who he was, I forget but it was definitely and invasion of my personal space and somewhat confrontational. I believe he smirked and continued walking up the stairs. Apparently he lived on the fourth floor - the floor above mine and this is the first time I saw the person in the building. One thing about this building is the walls breathe - meaning it's easy to hear people walking on the floor above or moving things around. As I entered my rental room it seemed so did also a person above me and started scuffling things around. This time instead of moving out again I decided to stick around for awhile like I stated earlier to see if I could shield from the directed energy assaults. The wire mesh stapled on the ceiling above wasn't something I tried right away, but it was after some weeks or months staying there. Many targeted individuals are curious about what material will work to alleviate some of the torment and be able to get some rest. The idea of the wire mesh is similar to the shielding that you see on a microwave oven door. I would say it did help a little but not much. I recall some targeted individuals stressing the importance of grounding anything metallic like a Faraday Cage or it will not be effective against the directed energy. Maybe other TI's reading this can try grounding their metallic shielding, but grounding wasn't something I tried. As time went on I went from sleeping on the bed to having two mattresses with plywood propped open at an angle with me lying on the floor underneath, wearing the army helmet saved from the previous apartment. I noticed there was a considerable difference in the amount of directed energy that could get through. I learned that obstructions like extra mattresses, bags of clothes, plywood piled on top of that, and putting more material between you and the person using the pain ray - lessons the effect of the directed energy. Later I learned this acts like a type of barrier or absorption against the RF. For awhile, I was able to get enough sleep but that did not last long. Then I felt bumping underneath my head while lying on the floor - like someone was positioning equipment below me on the second floor. Sure enough, the intensity of the electronic harassment increased again. It did not help that it was in the dead of the summer time and I had no air conditioning. For some strange reason sleeping with the Army helmet on started to feel comfortable but in reality the days where I could relax in a room I was paying for were over.

What It's Like To Cope/Live With Sleep Deprivation

During the early targeting days the electronic harassment was intense. I could feel the nerves in the side of my head or temple throbbing. When you're suffering from sleep deprivation you're looking for anywhere where you can get some sleep. Sleep deprivation is a common torture tactic and it can be caused by no-touch torture or what is also termed white torture. No-touch torture was mentioned in the CIA's 1963 KUBARK interrogation manual during the Cold War. I remember walking up the top of the stairs where there was a door to the top of the building and no other apartment doors. I saw an area where I could lay down on the floor trying to squeeze out a few hours of sleep. It was difficult, for one it was hot and then the thought occurred: what would happen if someone like the superintendent walked up the stairs to the roof and saw you there? Or the perpetrator knew you were there? So that was a no go. I would be walking down the street finding myself looking at the side of buildings, park benches, anywhere that looked like it was a safe place to take a nap. I actually tried sleeping on a park bench near Riverside Park on 145th street while the sun was setting and it was just starting to get dark. As I laid there I pretended to be asleep because I saw some neighborhood hoodlum staring at me from across the road, and he started opportunistically slowly walk toward my direction like he was going to do something. I quickly got up and said some not very nice words (you can fill in the blanks) but that quashed my efforts to take a nap on a park bench. It brought back memories of those trying times in 2006 when I first came to New York and had a short three month stint of becoming homeless, arriving at the Greyhound bus station at the Port Authority terminal on 42nd street with very little to no money and falling asleep in front of the Port Authority with pedestrians walking around. Then there was the time when I was homeless trying to sleep in a park in Brooklyn, New York. It was a park with a grassy hill with trees and a walk path was underneath. It was starting to get dark and I woke up as creepily, a man down a walk path stood in his tracks looking at me with a blank stare - like he wanted to do something; like he was a serial killer. He didn't look homeless or poor; was neatly dressed to blend in with society. I quickly got up and walked off. I remember during that homeless stint that I was so tired that objects would fall out of my hand. This also sometimes happen when I started suffering from sleep deprivation from being electronic harassed. A lot of people seem to not understand that one of the main issues with homelessness is safety and security, as well as privacy, finding a place to use the restroom - those more intimate moments. It's not easy to live on the streets, although I remember feeling happy when I was homeless that I did not have to go to a 9 to 5 job and the awkward interaction one has with co-workers. I saw a lot of miserable faces, people putting on their work outfits or professional attire and scurrying off to a job that they did not look forward to. I was glad that wasn't me, but the nomadic lifestyle didn't seem very sustainable and I knew that I would have to get back into the rat race like everyone else at some point.

The Navy Yard Shooter - "Insider Threat," "My ELF Weapon"

In 2013 there was news of an active shooter named Aaron Alexis termed the Navy Yard shooter. According to the news Aaron Alexis described electronic harassment that would build up to a psychotic break or his actions were an outcry of desperation because of physical torment he was allegedly going through. Some of what Alexis described very much reflected my own electronic harassment experience, like suffering from sleep deprivation. Alexis even tried seeking help for his sleep deprivation. Other aspects of Alexis case also reflected my harassment such as being stalked by his harassers when trying to move and being somewhat of a loner. Alexis appears to have had behavioral issues described as insubordinate according to descriptions of his military service in the Navy or work history. At the time he worked for a contractor. It makes you wonder if he was labeled an "insider threat" and part of some inside threat mitigation program by a private intelligence contractor who had access to directed energy devices. At the time, like in all mass shooting cases, the cop-out excuse or explanation by the media was mental health. The FBI concluded that his claims of electronic harassment were delusional which you'll later learn the media has used to described targeted individuals. Other notable active shooter cases where alleged targeting took place are Myron May or the Florida State shooter who thought he was being watched and Esteban Santiago, the Fort Lauderdale Airport shooter who claimed of hearing voices, mind control by the CIA after returning from service in Iraq. After the story about the Navy Yard Shooter broke, I posted that I thought it was the FBI using directed energy to YouTube videos commenting about the shooting. I did this while I was at work and as I was getting off work crossing the street on the northwest side of Union Square Park a car charged toward me crossing two lanes and tried to hug the corner where I would cross. I saw the driver was a dweeby or nerdy looking man with a determined expression on his face. I stepped back on the sidewalk at the right moment averting the hit-and-run attempt. My mother would described something similar while trying to cross the street in Pasadena, California. She described two men wearing dark clothing with sun glasses inside the car aiming straight for her.

The Long Distance Electronic Harassment From Cell Towers; Satellites?

At the same time all this was occurring in 2013, being harassed in the workplace, being hit on of the head or stomach while sitting in the lobby area, there was another type of electronic harassment while walking down the street in Manhattan. I would call this long distance electronic harassment. It was different than being electronic harassed at close range. In a rental room like the one I was staying at on 147th street you could tell someone was operating equipment, you could hear the person moving equipment around, selectively targeting a part of your body. The sensation was more intense. The long distance harassment usually focused on one part of the body - in this case it was my left ear. I could feel the hairs in my ear canal moving around, what I would call a bug crawling effect - all the while having the ringing in the ear. It was enough to be uncomfortable but not as intense as being targeted at close range where there was what I would call a sharp pain with a bruising to the touch afterward. Some targeted individuals have speculated that the directed energy is coming from satellites; others tend to believe it's from the RF antennas placed on top of buildings that shoot down signals to your phone. Specialized equipment has been set up so the antennas can be used as a pain weapon. Sometimes I wonder if the giant spire on top of One World Trade is a giant RF weapon or a secret weapon that can shoot a high energy laser if another plane approaches like 9-11 but I'm only being half serious when I write those thoughts. What I was experiencing was real and it was hard to avoid. I was a target being hit with this weaponry that most of the public was oblivious about. I would also feel it on the subway and I would wonder how this was possible. Once while walking at the subway platform at Times Square 42nd street, a day when I was being targeted hard I felt the skin in my face having spasms, as if this equipment is placed in high traffic sensitive areas (tourist traps; critical infrastructure) by homeland security.

Saw The Perp and He Got Spooked

Curiosity got the best of me and I had to see who was the person on the floor above dragging the equipment in the building on 147th street. The perpetrator's room was above so I put a small USB web can on some sticks like on a broom that were taped-together to see if I could make out anything from the window above. At first all I could make out was curtain and what appeared to be cardboard box concealing a part of the window, then there was a little opening in the curtain, but from what I made out it was not enough to reveal what was in the room, except I could make out a cot to the side of a room, which kind of made since if equipment was dragged on the floor, although I could not see the rest of the room if the perp or perps cleared out a bed or furniture, then I saw what looked like a cable, thinking it may be a coaxial cable used for some type equipment in my harassment – sometime later after analyzing the images and seeing lettering on the cable it turned out to be strings to an Under Armour Gym Sackpack. It was just so close to the webcam it looked like a coaxial cable. It appears someone put their gym bag close to the window. It just goes to show when doing surveillance you have to be careful not to jump to conclusions or one can discredit themselves appearing paranoid. I later found out that you can get in to trouble peeping into a window even if it is based on suspicion; you are not trying to invade privacy, so it's generally not a good idea, especially if you approach the authorities. At the time though, I wanted to capture evidence of the actual equipment being used, seeing what it was. I tried another time and the perpetrator above was aware, as the camera approached the window a hand pulled the curtains to the side and there was the face of the African American male who gave me the intimidating stare on the staircase as described earlier. As he pulled the curtains to the side he yelled, " I see you!" I was a bit startled and taken aback but now knew who the perpetrator was. I thought he may call the police on me but nothing happened. This is something I observed about the perpetrators over time. They don't really get the police involved. When I think about it that kind of makes sense, since if it is not a serious charge then I could request a police report to see who the accusers are using this equipment. Or they probably don't want the cops to see what they're actually doing even though the police may be aware of some type of homeland security/FBI activity, clandestine type stuff. The perpetrator at this time was starting to get scared. I think the pain ray harassment was supposed to get me out of the way in short order like a covert action but that did not happen. When I left the room like I was leaving, I could hear the perpetrator above put equipment away and proceed to shut his door and go down the stairs to exit the building. I decided next time I would pretend to leave by shutting my

door and listen for him to leave then follow behind. That
is exactly what happened, as he went down the stairs I
waited until he got far enough away and then exited the
apartment and proceeded to go down the stairs. I caught
up with him when he was in the hallway taking pictures
with my iPhone and proceeded to follow the perpetrator
as he went to the store. His hand was always in his pocket
knowing that I was trailing his position like he was
carrying a firearm. I knew that the electronic harassment
was a type of provocation. if the targeted individual
attacks then they are prepared to take you out, as if that
sort of thing is anticipated.

2013-summer 2014; 520 West 162 St #51 New York,
NY. 10032

I went further up in Upper Manhattan to Washington
Heights, New York to a new room rental. This room
rental did not end well, I was eventually told to leave. I
think the tenants got scared or got the wrong impression.
The tenant in this building was named Nuna and she was
a hispanic woman with two little girls. She did not seem
very friendly; maybe on guard because of previous room
renters. I got the impression she had trouble paying for
the apartment and may have been behind on bills. A
Latino man with a mustache would come by, I believe he
was her boyfriend but the father was no longer there. I'm

not sure of the exact details of her life but that was my impression and I sensed a bit of family disfunction. There was also a younger man who came across as a loser and a bit slow mentally in the room closest to the door. At first he was a bit testy when I moved in but then realized I kept to myself and stayed out of his way. The room I was renting was second from the door. This building too was about five stories tall and also did not have an elevator; it was a little rougher in appearance inside. Next to the building was a torn down lot where they were in the process of doing construction, building a new five story complex. There were a group of feral cats also staying in the empty lot. One could see my window from 162nd street since there was an empty lot. This building had another advantage - I was on the top floor. There was no one to drag equipment on the floor above mine. At first everything went well, like the previous room when first moving in - and then it became apparent that I was being hit with directed energy from below about two or three days later after moving in. I believe this happened at the previous building too, if you remember when I tried to sleep on the floor with the mattresses and plywood piled on top of me, to shield from the perpetrator dragging equipment above; but then came bumping underneath my head. So the perpetrators using this pain ray equipment can get on the floor above or below in a building, except now they only had access to the floor below and the directed energy was pointed upwards. Here the pain ray was still intense - again I would have to try and shield myself by putting material between me and the perpetrator. The pain ray was so intense a person could not stay in the room without some type of barrier or passive shielding - it easily passes through a floor or ceiling. I remember my stomach and head was targeted a lot. My sleeping position was facing down on the mattress - I rarely sleep on my back. During the stay at this building I decided to try other shielding methods. I purchased a thicker type of space blanket or mylar blanket at a camping/outdoor store and it helped a little, I forget the brand but it had a orange/reflective appearance. I found this was better than the cheap-thin disposable mylar blankets used in emergencies, it also lasted longer. Since the electronic harassment was intense and almost unbearable at times without any type of shielding I started just picking up stuff that I saw thrown out on the street like styrofoam, cardboard, thrown out window screening and probably other stuff and piled it below the bed, under the mattress to see if had any shielding effect. Also since it was getting cold, fall weather was approaching, I tried wearing winter hats when trying to sleep since the head was targeted a lot. One thing I found that was effective in shielding was a big laundry-bag full of clothes densely packed or thick material like blue jeans - It seemed to act as a type of absorption or it made it harder for the directed energy to penetrate. One thing new I did too in this room rental was purchase a TriField EMF Meter to try and gather some type of evidence of the actual directed energy. Would I be able to detect it?

Useless EMF Meters That Have Limited Range

When I was on 162nd street, I tried gathering evidence by buying survey meters or what are called EMF meters like a TriField Meter. These type of measuring devices are consumer grade products that you see people use on a Ghost Hunter TV show or people on the internet who try to measure suspected harmful radiation from smart meters - some would say they are just novelty products. The frequency range is a bit limited due to the cost although I believe there are better options out there today including the newer TriField meters. I believe the TriField only had the range of a microwave oven when set to the microwave band setting - it didn't reach high band millimeter wave like Active Denial System frequency, that required specialized equipment with probes attached. The TriField also had two magnetic settings and one for electrical field. Magnetic field reading measure current and electric field readings measure voltage. Of course the radio setting measures microwave or RF. To measure something like Raytheon's Active Denial it would take specialized equipment that measures mmWave in the high-band range but purchasing probes and such equipment would be really expensive. I also bought other products from a company called Less EMF that sells electromagnetic shielding material to consumers. Many people are concerned about the harmful effects of wireless signals or smart meters etc. Whether this is unfounded or not there are customers for that type of product. Some people claim that they suffer from Electromagnetic hypersensitivity (EHS). Another product I bought detected electromagnetic interference by creating a hum when it detects something electrical like an electrical outlet or a light fixture where there is electricity. I later learned you could use a portable AM radio set on noise between two stations to do the same thing. Higher-end equipment like survey meters with probes and spectrum analyzers were expensive and required a certain level of technical expertise (this type of equipment would have been more ideal in my situation). These are used by the professionals around RF equipment. I did purchase one device by Narda from Ebay I believe it was called the Nardalert S3 or maybe an older model of that variety. I then sent it off to Narda in New York to have it calibrated and some weeks later got it back with a certificate of calibration. The Nardalert S3 looked like a big pager for people who worked around RF equipment; a worker would clip it on to a belt to detect harmful RF. It would make a beep or tone if harmful RF levels were detected. The problem with the Narda unit is it worked with old PC software in order to adjust the settings and also to see a log of readings. It was an older model to the company's more current product line. At the time I just had a MacBook, not a PC with the software needed to see a log of readings. Once at work I was wearing the Narda and saw short spike in the LED indicator but the same reading never was replicated. After having not much luck with the Narda unit I later re-sold it on Ebay. I tested the TriField Meter in the room and was not able to pick up the directed energy frequency in the microwave band but may have indirectly picked up a byproduct of the equipment being used when I set it on the floor where I was laying on the bed and switched it to magnetic range. The needle on the TriField dial started moving as it detected something. Was this a light fixture underneath or some type of equipment positioned underneath my location? I recall I was unable to detect the same signal when I put the TriField on the floor again sometime later. I also made a discovery, while the activity was strong I put my ear to the floor since I was on the top floor and knew the person using the equipment was on the floor underneath, and could hear a low modulating sound that went 'whump…whump…whump…" at regular intervals. This is a sound that I would be able to record in later room rentals using a piezo-electric microphone or pick-up mic. I believe it was related to whatever equipment was being used. I stayed at this location (on 162nd Street) until the following Summer. One interesting thing was the perpetrator's room below mine had the window always half open with the curtains drawn, but I think it was always like that even when I moved in. The electronic harassment was so intense during times of strong activity I banged the upper portion of the perpetrators window using a broom with my arm and chest out of my window, banging the window below and then the window appeared semi broken or cracked. There was another time I was so mad I yanked on a cable from the roof that went into the perpetrators apartment - and I heard a TV fall over and out came a recorder with an SD card attached to the cable. I was afraid that I would be accused of theft if I kept it to see what was on it so I let the cable drop to the side of the building. Sometimes I regret not seeing what was on the SD card - it makes me wonder if my electronic harassment was being recorded. That would have been a smoking gun. I also put a web cam onto a stick and tried to look into the window. The curtains made it hard to see what was exactly in the room using the web cam, I did make out something rectangular shaped like the backside of a window air conditioner but nothing really conclusive. Interestingly enough you would think all of these incidents would have the neighbors calling the cops but like the perpetrator in the previous room who saw my peep cam - nothing happened. The tenant named Nuna who I paid rent to I believed suspected something. The spring or summer arrived and I don't remember if I was coming or going but I saw the building superintendent replacing the window on the room below. The superintendent had placed a large drawer behind him so no one looking at the window could see what's inside the room. I waited until he was done and then saw him on the first floor after he left the apartment. I asked what was inside that room and he just gave me a stare and did not say anything. I got the impression he saw something and was instructed or not willing to talk; he looked upset. Around that time there was a dispute with the tenant over the restroom that seemed to be always occupied. Someone misconstrued my words to mean something I did not say during an argument and I was told to move. I obliged not wanting any trouble while getting electronic harassed. I also knew the woman had two girls. In the previous apartment the woman there had a small boy. I know there is a government element to this harassment and it is a bit shocking that they would torment a person with the pain ray when other families are around, just to make money from counter-terror spending or the justification of a controversial weapon that has to be used out of the public's eye. Whatever politician in congress, governor, mayor, or whoever signed off on this program it seems a bit irresponsible. A person being tormented, harassed, suffering from sleep deprivation - you don't know how they will react, they could snap like Aaron Alexis. Why would you do that with women, children, and families in the same dwelling? Not only is the technology evil and cruel but the people using it, seem to have a lack of regard for life around them. I know there are probably more than one perpetrator in a building - a team effort and the targeted person is on 24/7 watch, but I just don't see them being able to stop a target who snaps from doing something bad. The amount of stupidity and the levels of abuse in government never ceases to amaze me. These are the same people who will argue that being more transparent about what technology they are testing may help the terrorist if revealed - yet they put people's lives in harms way. Would you want to live in a building where a person was being tortured with directed energy week after week? Would you want your children living there - on the same apartment floor? As I moved out of the apartment on 162nd street the two little girls were running up the stairs laughing as I was painfully carrying my stuff down the steps. The empty lot next to it now had construction as a new building was going up and a construction crew was hammering away. Someone moved the feral cats down below where they keep the trash. I found another rental room through a rental room agency a little further south on 156th street.

How the Perps Monitor the Person In The Other Room

I noticed the perpetrator would make adjustments like increasing the directed energy when I tried to shield from it or tried to put more obstructions in the way. It's like they could see your radar or infrared body image and with the equipment they were using to see how much pain ray to apply. I often wondered how the perpetrator using the equipment could see the targeted person in the other room. I later learned about see-through technology like hand-held units placed against the wall to see whats inside a building were first used by the military. Most people are familiar with millimeter wave body scanners at the airport. There have been articles recently about using RF to see through a wall. See-through body scanners were tested on the public at New York's Penn Station using "passive millimeter wave" technology by a company called QinetiQ. The person's image on a screen looks similar to a thermal image with objects that can be seen concealed underneath their clothing. There are now body scanners that use Terahertz too. Ironically, Raytheon's pain ray also uses millimeter waves. Another possibility in how the perpetrators are able to see the targeted individual is hidden cameras like a small pinhole camera. Although I'm not an expert on spy equipment. I'm sure these days someone could put something really small and undetectable in a room. I tend to believe though it was the see-through technology that was being used with my electronic harassment.

08/2014; 520 W 156 St Apt 51 NY, NY.

It was now the year 2014. I survived a year of intense electronic harassment. This new rental room I found was on the top floor again. It was another five story building and I was on the fifth floor. This building had only stairs, no elevator like the last building and the room was rented out by a couple who had a small boy. The father was a taxi cab driver. He may have been affected by the Uber craze that was hitting the New York Taxi cab drivers in the wallet. I got the impression they only wanted to rent a room for money and I wasn't that welcome but then again they had a small child. My room was small, I believe it had a TV with remote and a small little shelf or drawer where I put my music gear. I forget when the directed energy started up again but I would say about two or three days after moving in. I made an interesting observation though that would later be observed in a future room rental. Shortly after securing my room rental I observed a young adult person in the apartment below mine reluctantly moving out carrying luggage. He didn't seem too pleased and was complaining. As the directed energy started up coming from the room below mine, I tried to be as discreet as possible in putting shielding material underneath the bed such as aluminum pans. The thicker type orange/silver space blanket that I purchased at a camping outdoor store was used on the mattress. I also purchased a cheap EMF Meter online and tested it out walking around the neighborhood. It wasn't very good but when a subway train would go by as you were waiting on the subway platform you could see a spike in EMF readings. It had a simple graphical interface comprising of LED lights that would light up when close to an EMF source. While the directed energy intensified from underneath I placed the device on the floor and the LED light started blinking but I couldn't tell if it also blinked if low on batteries (if I recall from reading the instruction manual). I recorded this activity using my laptop camera. Temptation got the best of me and I decided to put a web cam on a stick with the really long USB cable and tried peering in the window below me. I could barely make out furniture but the curtain was usually concealed. Nothing really new happened in this room rental compared to the others and my stay was not long but I did confront the neighbor downstairs. Once while passing by the neighbor's apartment below where the perp would have been, a woman had the door open, she was cooking. At first I didn't pay any mind even though it was tempting to run through the open door and have a look in the room below mine. The floor plan in this building was as you walked through the front door there was the kitchen area connected to bedrooms - one to the side and others straight ahead down a hallway. The room below mine would have been a short distance by running through the kitchen from the front door. I decided not to because I also knew the perpetrator was armed and would probably shoot me if there. I also knew I was getting hit hard with the directed energy and there was a reason - it was a type of provocation. Another time going up the stairs I noticed the door open with the woman cooking and she was with another person having a conversation. This time I had the courage to make my way in the apartment a little bit and ask her who was in the room below mine. I may have explained I was getting electronic harassed when she questioned who I was and then she shut down and told me to take some steps back and had nothing to say to me as she shut the door - almost like she was instructed to say that. My stay here ended abruptly. As I would go down

the stairs I would turn the door knob where the perp
underneath me was staying, I thought I might as well
mess with their heads. Well, turning the door knob was
enough for the tenant that I was renting a room from to
tell me to leave once she got wind of it. One recurring
thing is there is always cameras observing the apartments.
i.e. surveillance. Even something small like turning a
door knob will be detected and played back on video.
Whether this is the tenants complaining to management or
it has to do with security precautions by the perps - I do
not know, but again the police were never involved. I got
the impression the apartment downstairs liked their
freedom of having the door open when they cooked and
were really neighborly like most Latino people are. They
did not like the perpetrators in their apartment who were
uninvited guest. Seeing me leave so the perpetrators
would vacate the building is something I also observed in
the next room rental. People would rather have their
freedom than have these perpetrators throwing their
weight around around. It was my time to make an
awkward departure and look for another room using the
room rental agency.

11/2014; 3671 Broadway #41 New York, NY. 10031

I moved to this building located on Broadway, It was
closer to my old neck of the woods in Hamilton Heights.

It was also located near the historic Trinity Church graveyard. The room was not on the top floor but the fourth floor so there was a room above and below me. A mid-aged woman was renting out a room that faced the fire escape and street. She appeared divorced; her daughter was married to a man who shared a small room near the restroom. Once they started banging on the restroom while I was taking a dump and complained my excrement smelled. I was sure to use air freshener after that. I don't think they worked; they claimed to go to college I forget but they seemed (careful not to use the word ghetto) immature. There seemed to be a lot of yelling amongst the women in the house. This area was a bit troubled or rough around the edges. I believe there was latino gang activity. A young Latino rapper was shot near the building standing next to a bodega in the early morning hours while I was living there although I did not see it happen but there were always young hoodlum type people hanging out front. What I also remember about this place is the hoodlums out front would play the same rap song over and over again really loud which was quite annoying. This room rental was basically, the same routine as in the other rental rooms where the electronic harassment started up again after two or three days where it was at a hight intensity level. I remember I was mostly targeted in the head and the stomach. What got me in trouble here is the electronic harassment got the best of me and I had to go up the fire escape and take a peak into the window above. An old woman walking down the hallway saw me peeking into the window and let out a yell. I could hear someone opening a drawer and bumping equipment around above me while I was getting electronic harassed. After the woman in the apartment above was startled a man came down and gave me an ultimatum. He told me to leave and he wouldn't call the police. I got the impression that whoever was in the room using the directed energy equipment was an unwelcome guest. They seem to be able to get into these apartments whether the tenants want them there or not. This points to people in a position of authority. At this point I was tempted to tell him to go ahead. The pattern of getting physically abused and being on the run having to hall all my belongings including musical equipment was getting old but I also knew in this case the law was not on my side. So I gave in, but instead of moving to another room rental in New York I took some vacation time at work and decided go back to Dallas, Texas and try to find work there. If it didn't work out I could always take a plane back and return to my security job. I made a deal with a friend who still lived in the Dallas area to hold on to some of my music equipment that I would ship as I tried to make the transition moving to another state.

12/2014; 422 N Lancaster Ave #4B. Dallas, Texas. 75203

I found this place in Oak Cliff, Dallas by looking for room rental agencies similar to what I was doing in Manhattan. Dallas, Texas did not have a lot of room rental agencies. It was either find a roommate in the classifieds or get an apartment lease. However I did see a classified for one room agency and it was located in an old apartment complex close to Downtown Dallas. I went to see a person named Al Turner and payed a deposit and a weeks rent for a room in Oak Cliff, Texas. His operation reminded me of a boarding house type place taking in mostly poor people who may be on disability or recovering addicts. Al referred me to a two story apartment that was being revamped but there was still some rooms available. I got on the freeway down I35E exiting to Oak Cliff, Texas that is the southern west portion of Dallas near downtown and found the apartment. This area was traditionally African American with lots of small wooden houses. There is also a large Mexican American population not too far away where Lee Harvey Oswald hid out at the Texas Theater - Its still there as a type of historical marker. I went by and saw the place Al Turner referred me to off Lancaster Avenue and spoke to a person named Cecil Green who was and African American with a Texas drawl. He was a native to the area and was overseeing tenants as well as construction. I asked whether the area was dangerous and he said not really if I keep to myself. Also on a humorous note people would take their laundry and wash it at an apartment down the street when I asked about a laundry mat. I was shown a room that I would share with an elderly African American man who mostly stayed in bed. I can't say he was bed ridden because he would get up with a cane and walk around but a caretaker or nurse type woman would come by on occasion to look after him. There was also the strong smell of urine because of his health condition. I was shown a kitchen area and small bathroom that was to be shared with the elderly man who was already staying there. My room was a small room next to the old man's with a small mattress, a closet, and some trash lying around. I decided to take it since it was cheap and required no lease even though the place was a bit run down which didn't seem to bother me. Also while there in Oak Cliff I returned the rental car and purchased a 1995 Toyota Corolla which turned out to be a mistake. Toyota's are usually good cars but this one had seen better days with very high mileage and was on its last legs. It seemed the automatic transmission was about to go out and was slow switching into gears. I payed I believe $1200 for it. The used car lots in the area make their money off of financing not so much outright selling a used car. I also found a place to purchase cheap car insurance and put a downpayment on that. It seemed like I was settling down in the area and was going to stay awhile, even though I was technically on a two-week vacation from my job in New York. Well several days pass and one day while I was walking into the apartment there was a latino American looking man staring at me from the stairway going to the second floor with a smirk on his face. I didn't say anything and proceeded to enter the apartment. The apartment with my room was on the first floor or bottom floor. Above me I could hear furniture moving around like someone was in an hurry to move the furniture in the room. I exited the apartment to try and see what was going on and out came a younger African American woman holding a suitcase looking visually annoyed. I believed she said she had to move but was very mum and would not say much when I tried to question her why. Sure enough, I believe that night here came the dragging of equipment onto of me with what sound like something metallic or hard being dropped over my head with the same sensation of the directed energy pain-ray. Earlier that day I was out and about and was able to secure a job through a temporary employment service - it was a job moving medical equipment to rooms in the new Parkland Hospital. Interestingly enough while at the employment agency (forget the name) that was in a skyscraper near I75 & 635 in North Dallas, near Richardson, I had to do a background check while I waited there. The person doing the screening returned but his demeanor had changed. I got the impression the person doing the employment screening either saw something or was told something that didn't put me in a very good light. Sure enough, it's like the perpetrator above me knew that I had a job the next day that required a certain amount of walking-manual labor since my feet were targeted and were pretty bruised up when I had to go to the job the following morning. The sensation of the pain ray weapon is of course what I would call a sharp pain like a bee-sting or burning, followed by a bruising sensation to the skin afterward. I went to the job and was put with a bunch of other men who were mostly from poor urban backgrounds, we were divided in groups at the new Parkland Hospital building, playing scavenger hunt looking for rooms with numbers using a building schematic to put equipment in. The job only lasted about 4 hours but it was a bit uncomfortable to walk because of the pain ray harassment. I believe that was the last day of this temporary job and the employment agency never called me back. I forget how long I stayed in that apartment complex on Lancaster Avenue but I did stay at a hotel not too far away near I35E I believe the last day I was there. I remember before leaving helping the elderly man with his TV remote and telling him that I was returning to New York - he seemed surprised. I could tell he would go through my room when I was gone, looking for money but I didn't hold it against him - his days appeared numbered and so did mine, it seemed. I took some photos of the place before I left and even went upstairs to listen to see if I could hear anything coming from the apartment. I could only hear some people talking like a man and a woman but couldn't make out what they were saying. One concern with living there is many people have guns, Texas is a big gun state, so trying to snoop around and gather evidence didn't seem very wise. When my vacation was about to end I learned something - the electronic harassment was not just in New York but I would be followed if moving to another state, at least in Texas, and I know California where a family member was targeted. Who actually approves the harassment - I don't know. Some have speculated Fusion Centers, The FBI, private contractors who are actually doing it. Do they need to go to a judge to get approval or is it just done indiscriminately. I could only speculate but it didn't seem like a small operation. Before leaving I had to retrieve my music gear that I mailed to a friend living in Dallas. He was a bit reluctant giving it back, and in fact pretty much avoiding me when I was there, claiming a busy schedule but I think there may have been some money issues and he was planning to move. He tried going in business for himself after quitting an IT job at Fossil (the watch company) that is located in North Texas some years back citing new management. As funny irony would have it. I also gave him vinyl records before moving to New York in 2006 and saw some of the same records while browsing the used vinyl section at Half Priced Books at Northwest Highway. Half Priced books is similar to a book store called The Strand in New York. I could tell they were my records because the type of music wasn't very common and I recognized the wear and tear on the record jackets. I also remember him telling me he goes there to dump off CDs for cash. Now was the issue of ditching the car since a refund wasn't an option. A salvage yard would only give me $300 but after inquiring at a Pawn Shop I was told about a Mexican American car repair shop near Love Field Airport that sells used cars on commission. That seemed like the better option. I went to the place explaining I had to move. The owner was very friendly and I think even drove me to a Dart Rail Station after agreeing to sell the car. I went back to see Al Turner who ran the boarding house/ room rental operation out of an apartment complex and got my deposit back explaining things just didn't work out. He didn't seem too pleased and didn't seem to know what was going on. The superintendent overseeing repairs to the apartment on Lancaster Avenue I believe knew something based on his reaction when I told I was leaving - he had a type of smirk on his face. An observation I made while getting electronic harassed is the superintendent's of buildings usually know that something is happening. Do they know exactly what is going on with the electronic harassment I am unsure but it appears someone is able to throw their weight around to get inside the apartment rooms either above or below where the target is staying. Before my flight departed I mailed back my music equipment in two big boxes at a Post Office near downtown Dallas. I still had a PO Box in New York. I was a bit sad I could not move back to Dallas and had to return to New York to my security job where I was a guinea pig to this directed energy weaponry but at least New York had mass transit and I didn't have to worry about a car.

2015 - Going to Doctors To Get Checked Out

Maybe a year or two after the pain ray harassment began I started going to doctors using my health insurance at work. I went to a cardiologist woman near central park when my chest was being targeted. When I arrived I got the impression she wasn't a serious doctor and just prescribed meds to the rich in the area. She listened to my heart and then put me on a treadmill and made me walk for a few minutes. Didn't seem particularly fond of me because I wasn't her usual customer. She made me go nearby to a lab to get a blood sample taken. I had to ask if the needles were clean because the people taking the blood samples looked like they just got out of a medical billing and nursing for-profit school. Like all things New York the place seemed kind of dirty. The cardiologist subscribed some feel good drugs but I didn't bother because I know America has a serious drug problem. I did a follow up appointment because blood samples were taken in a lab. She said my thyroid seemed to be off or high. I recall that the thyroid is especially susceptible to radiation exposure. I also went to see an eye doctor when my eyes were being targeted. In fact because of all the pain I went through I think one eye is slightly crooked. It was one of those places where they also sell you glasses. He put a device in my eye to have a close look and it was inconclusive. Then I went to see a cancer doctor who always advertises non invasive cancer treatment on the radio in New York. If you listen to the same AM radio station that plays CoastToCoast Am in New York you probably know what Doctor I am referring to. He had a big photo of former Mayor Giuliani on his wall. I believe I told him about the electronic harassment and cancer concerns but I don't think he seemed to care much. He suggested that I could get an MRI then handed me a bunch of promotional material about his show - all of it ugly useless like junk mail. I think he believed that people were actually interested in hearing him talk on a paid radio infomercial and he was proud of his show. The people at the receptionist desk were eager to get my insurance info like hungry sharks. I made my way to the hospital for an MRI of my skull. I remember the ear ringing was especially strong as I was in the MRI machine lying down flat on my back faced upwards like it interfered with what I suspect is an electronic tag placed deep n my ear canal. I did a follow up appointment with the cancer doctor and the MRI didn't detect anything abnormal. I also went to take a physical. I was told that nothing was wrong with me but I was morbidly obese and should job more often; control the intake of food by counting calories. I went to see an ear doctor because of the ear ringing. Nothing was found to be the matter. As I was going down the elevator a man with a cane told the story of going to see the wrong doctor and he thinks he's being experimented on. I told him based on my experience, I'm not surprised or I know the feeling. One thing I did not do, or should do is a psychological examination since that is the go-to excuse the police and mainstream media use to try to deny electronic harassment or the abuse of directed energy is happening. Then again, would police take it seriously? They would probably still involuntary commit you following protocol like so many other TI's. My mother too went to see doctors regarding her harassment. Early on I think it was a general examination after being frightened. Then when her feat were being targeted so she would have a hard time walking my big sister took her to see a foot doctor, then more recently a doctor about her legs when her legs were being targeted. Then my Mom told the story of how a creepy nurse showed up one day to take blood samples and she had a circular red mark on her arm afterward. One downside of being targeted with the pain compliance weapons and being told nothing is wrong with you when you go see a doctor is one could have pain not related to the pain ray harassment. A recent example is going to see a dentist and being reminded that he told me about a cavity two years ago and asked if my tooth was throbbing - now I needed a root canal. Then you're kind of weary about having a procedure done because of the horror stories from other targeted individuals about being tagged or having a chip implanted. I almost forgot that I also went to see a dermatologist about a skin condition on my leg. The dermatologist woman looked at my leg with fascination and told me it was a type of dermatitis. I asked her what the cause was but she said it remains unknown and there wasn't much she could do. Upon further investigation the rash on my leg very much resembled a condition called radiation dermatitis. It's caused by radiotherapy. i.e. exposure to radiation. The dermatitis condition started in Texas when I was getting the more crude form of electronic harassment. During the early days of the electronic harassment it was still inflamed, in recent years it has started to clear up.

01/2015 to 02/27/16 - 558 West 164th Street #6H

Upon returning to New York landing at Laguardia Airport, I remember getting on the subway train after taking a city bus from the airport and heading back to Washington Heights to a room rental agency. I was sent to a room on 164th street. This new rental room I found was on the top floor again. It was a six story building. This building had an elevator so it was easier to transport my belongings. There was an older woman there who watched the place. Her kids appeared to be grown and had left the nest; were living elsewhere. Her husband was also old and was not living there. He was involved in little league baseball and the family pictures were in the living room. My room was not by the front door but down the hall close to the kitchen. The floor layout was shaped like an L. It was a long hallway that hooked right as you open the front door. The room was small and square shaped with I believe one window. It had a little rack with a small TV and a small portable fridge that I never used. I still did not give up on my music even though I was getting tortured. It was like Maslow's Hierarchy of Needs - I needed self-actualization, even though my basic needs and psychological needs were under attack. I believe the first few nights there after moving in the summer and feeling exhausted I was able to get some rest. With shielding I was able to get four-to-five-hour sleep but always seemed to feel tired. So did my family member who was being hit in California. At my room on 164th street I again became a hoarder, looking for cheap material to use as shielding. It seemed every time I moved to a new room rental older junk used as shielding would be thrown out to the curve with all the other building garbage. By that time it was pretty beat up and not practical to bring with me to a new place; I never leaved old junk behind for the tenant to see like wire mesh or junk found on the street out of fear I would be reported for suspicious activity when in reality I was merely trying to defend myself from extrajudicial type abuse. In the room on 164th street I tried to step up my shielding methods by purchasing more specialized shielding material. After hearing a program by Roger Tolces, a private investigator from Chicago who investigated electronic harassment cases on with CoastToCoast AM or on an archived show that he appeared on on the internet I learned of RF shielding material by a company called ECCOSORB. If I recall correctly, there was a story of a rich person being microwaved and had a casket insulated with ECCOSORB - that's where the person would sleep to escape the electronic harassment. So I purchased some used ECCOSORB material online. Two varieties. Both came in a box as looking square tiles. One box had thin squares that had a sandpaper texture. The other box were thicker with a more rubbery feel, I believe it was polyurethane. I placed these underneath the bed and I laid down. I put the thicker variety underneath my head and immediately I noticed the directed energy was less severe. I don't think the perpetrator below me was too happy. I felt bumping around and banging below me. It was a strange sensation to neutralize the pain beam. I could feel the directed energy around me but it did not really inflict pain - more like a tingling sensation. I kind of chuckled and laughed a little bit falling asleep. My adulation did not last long though, the perpetrator or perpetrators figured out what ECCOSORB sheets I was using and adjusted the frequency or amped the power because the pain sensation returned a day or so later. I believe they did turn up the juice or power because when using the ECCOSORB material I got the impression the directed energy was more intense. The thicker rubbery looking ECCOSORB sheets I got though always seem to offer some protection so I used those around my head. The thinner ones that looked like sand paper was not as effective. It must be pointed out that ECCOSORB is not the only brand of RF absorbing material on the market and it's not really intended for consumer use but more for the electronics and defense industry like in an Anechoic Chamber, and its very expensive. Using ECCOSORB was a confirmation that what I was being hit with was indeed RF - I was being microwaved harassed with the pain ray weapon Raytheon developed or the smaller pain ray weapons the National Institute of Justice was developing that was described in those old WIRED Magazine articles from 2008. I also at the time used aluminum cooking sheets placed under my bed along with the thinner sand paper looking ECCOSORB sheets thinking it would be a compliment but the pain ray was still intense.

Audio Reconnaissance; Sousveillance

During that time at 164th street I also started gathering evidence in the form of audio. I purchased a piezo electric microphone or contact microphone. Like in the previous room rental on the top floor I could place my ear on the floor and hear the low modulating sound that went "whump…whump…whump…" at regular intervals. These types of microphones are used in acoustic instruments and the audio signal usually goes through an amplifier. I already had music recording equipment so all I needed to do is hook up the audio cable to my recording equipment and amp the signal. Sure enough, after applying a little EQ I was able to hear the "whump…whump…whump…" sound and record it. I could also hear what sounded like someone walking up a ladder to the ceiling of the room below. It seemed when the electronic harassment was turned up strong the "whump…whump…whump…" sound turned into an angry swarm of bees as it became more revved up. I concluded since I heard the sound in multiple rental rooms, was able to record it with audio equipment, and it changed with the intensity of the harassment - that it was somehow related to the directed energy equipment being used to harass me. In one recording a person could be heard saying "here comes the sonar bounce" and some thumping could be heard close-by before the microphone was disabled. At a TI protest I attended in Washington D.C. I told a TI from North Carolina about what I heard listening in and he said it was a resonator and an ultrasonic weapon (USW). I was skeptical if USW was being used but recalled purchasing some acoustic sound absorbing foam for my music and having some good results using it as shielding. Something similar that looks like acoustic sound absorbing foam but for RF absorption is used in anechoic chambers.

Approaching NYPD - Very Defensive, Not A Good Outcome

While living in the room rental on164th street I believed I had sufficient evidence to approach law enforcement - at least it was worth a shot (no pun). I knew from experience though, being ignored when trying to report it to the FBI

and my mother shunned after calling the police in
Monrovia, California - that what I was experiencing may
be extrajudicial in nature and the police would be of no
help. I went to the 33rd Precinct and walked into the
station, maybe I was too bashful and did not word things
correctly but it became clear the cops were unwilling to
help, even formed a huddle (there is a term for this police
tactic) and tried to brush off my claim as not very serious;
a female cop said she would come by; one cop warned I
should be careful in what I say to them; one cop asked
what laws were being broken? The police have a point, a
person can easily incriminate themselves especially of
you are not on their good side. No cop ever came by. The
laws being enforced are designed for petty criminals not
so much abuse by your own government. My policy
toward cops is to always ignore them. If I see a cop
parked on the side of the road or patrolling the subway I
go about my business like they aren't there. I have
nothing against cops, I view them sort of like security
guards but also realize that my electronic harassment
represents an abusive part of our system. It's wrong on so
many levels like laws against stalking, harassment, and
assault; but directed energy also has the plausible
deniability factor. If the activity is government sanctioned
behavior kept out of the public's eye will police really
help you? So far researching targeted individuals who
have been electronically harassed I have yet to read a
story about a so called hero cop or the swat team braking
down a door and busting a Blackwater type company for

abusing directed energy devices against targeted citizens. It's more like a person is involuntary institutionalized after approaching police with their electronic harassment claims. Later after moving from New York City in 2020 I concluded I was on a terrorist watch-list after interaction with cops during traffic stops or cops pulling away and just driving off after reading my plates. This supports the theory of Federal involvement like secretive Fusion Centers. Being tracked state to state and cops can see that you are watch-listed (non-investigative subject) receiving instructions how to proceed.

The Perp Stooges at 164th Street

On 164th street I believed I saw the perpetrators, at least entering and exiting the apartment below mine, I also used my faithful webcam to have a peek in the window even though I really shouldn't be doing that. The room looked like a dump - it was messy with cups, socks, and garbage laying all over the place. I saw a bed; a tv on top of a counter; a closet but could only partially make out what was inside the room. Later I saw something that looked like a sex toy. That is important because it relates to what I would later hear coming from the apartment that seemed shocking. I could go to the kitchen and see if the room below mine had the light on or if the curtains were open. The webcam didn't really pick up anything conclusive. One person looked like the actor Joe DeRita who played Curly on The Three Stooges. He had a bald shaved head and The Three Stooges actor's face. I learned a female who always wore military bun hairdo and reading glasses was his mother. They sounded like they were from Brooklyn judging from the accent after hearing them speak. There was an older man who looked kind of like Larry from The Three Stooges because he had a patch of curly hair on each side of his head. His hair was white, I thought maybe he was in his 60s. When I first saw him he looked like he was from California the way he was dressed wearing Converse type shoes. He also had a mustache. Once following the older man up the elevator I stopped to watch him open the door to the apartment below mine, he turned to stare at me with a straight face and had one hand in his pocket like he was concealing a firearm, exactly like the African American male I followed from the room rental on 147th street that was in the room above mine where I heard equipment being dragged around. There was one incident where I caught the bald person who looked like the Curly actor from The Three Stooges at the same time in the elevator and I pretended to talk on the phone, I said "Yes, I see him now, I want you to cut off his head" as the Curly looking person was stepping out of the elevator, he turned around angrily and exclaimed, "I heard what you said, You're going to cut off my head, cut off my head?!" I told him I was having a private conversation and continued to my floor. Another experience that was somewhat disturbing was I was in my room rental apartment alone and staring out the kitchen window at the room below mine then all of the sudden I hear a woman yell "get off me, get off me!!! stop! stop!" and she started screaming, it went on for awhile. So I went downstairs and knocked on the door thinking there may have been a rape, at first no one answer, and then I heard the woman say "Answer the door it may be the police." The bald headed Curly looking guy opened the door and I told him what I heard. I forget what he said but it was something like nothing was the matter and then slammed the door. During the end of my stay here I would bounce a ball on the floor to taunt the perpetrator below. I guess they thought that was a good idea because the same thing would be done by the perpetrator on the floor above in a future room rental. The 164th street room rental ended because I threw some yogurt or soda at the door of the apartment below as I was leaving during a time of strong electronic harassment activity and I was told it was caught on camera. I think this was the only room rental where I tried to explain I was being electronic harassed. It was from the grown daughter of the tenant who spoke on the tenants behalf because she spoke better English. What's strange is no one ever called the cops. This was becoming a familiar pattern. One thing I will say in my defense is if you are getting electronic harassed real hard it really does take a certain amount of restraint to just take the abuse and not to retaliate. If this was a physical assault you have the right to defend yourself from a violent action. These

people who use directed energy may be in the other room
but it is the same as being physically assaulted - it's just
the police will not have your side because it is a very
difficult thing to prove. This is one of the hardest things
to cope with when it comes to directed energy assaults.

02/27/2016 to 2020- 393 Edgecombe Ave Apt. 32. New
York, NY. 10031

Edgecombe avenue is where I stayed the longest, and of
course the same thing as the other rooms would happen.
After a period of time maybe two or three days here came
the bumping and dragging of equipment over my head
and the sound of opening and shutting of drawers. I
started to use the thicker variety of ECCOSORB material
in an unconventional way. By this time the thicker
ECCOSORB was having some issues, some of it was
falling apart. What I did was use plastic tape and taped it
around a plastic waste basket that would fit over my head.
The waste basket was more rectangular shaped instead of
the cylindrical variety because the cylindrical type will
roll, the rectangular lies flat on the bed when you rest
your head inside. Then after the ECCOSORB tiles that
were tapped all around the plastic waste basket, I put a
layer of aluminum cooking sheets around it. Know this
can be tricky because metal cooking sheets can cut your
skin, so I rolled tape around them. Then I used some thick

material like blue jeans around all that. I found that doing
layers around the waste basket worked the best. The
perpetrator using the directed energy of course turned up
the power so it was more intense but at least it was a little
protection. I taped some of the cheaper Mylar blanket or
emergency blanket on the ceiling above my bed. I found
that it did help a little. When I had on the plastic waste
basket over my head to sleep with the layer of
ECCOSORB it wasn't full proof but it was enough where
I was able to fall asleep. The perpetrator then started
targeting the mouth, body, and feet. I also felt my
stomach being hit and some bumping underneath my bed
like there were perpetrators above and below. By this
time I gave up on using EMF meters or survey meters. It
seems that the more expensive variety was required. I
mailed them to my father in Italy who was into
electronics and junk.

Photographed A Woman Perp Holding a Gun In Window;
Covert Action Attempt

While at 393 Edgecombe, I would sometimes crawl out
the window to the fire escape and run up the fire escape
steps real fast to have a look-see in the room above but it
was only a short glance. Unlike the room rental on
Broadway I would only do a short glance and not stare in
front of the window that long so someone wouldn't get

frightened. I would also wait until there appeared to be no activity. Peering into the room it looked like the equipment being used was put away out of sight when the perpetrator was not there. I always heard a drawer opening and closing. When I was in my room and the perpetrator was there it always sounded like equipment was being set up and shuffled around, but the perpetrators eventually caught-on that I would try to go up the fire escape. They were setting up a trap. During the summer the window of the perpetrator's room was always a little open, almost like to tempt me to go up the fire escape. One hot summer evening I crawled out onto the fire escape and used my hands to mimic a walking motion up the fire escape steps, then I sneaked back into my rental room and proceeded to quietly exit the apartment going out to the street holding up my iPhone taking video footage of the room above mine. In the window was a short woman with her hair tied into a bun and with one arm stretched out had a gun pointed down the fire escape stairs and with the other hand appeared to be looking at a screen or tablet like there was a video feed. The perpetrator woman kept her position until noticing I was standing in the street taking video and pulled her head ducking out of sight in embarrassment. The video footage I took shows that the purpose of the targeting is provocation. When the targeted individual tries to attack (fight or flight response) because of the harassment, the perp will then shoot claiming self defense - like a legal killing or covert action. Why would the government do this? I guess it depends who you make mad, it could be counter-intelligence, my UFO research may have been enough in light of the Pentagon's UFO Threat study. This is why targeted individuals have to become extra cautious in how they approach things. Doing something out of anger or impulse may be a death sentence. How many people have been killed by electronic harassment while trying to retaliate I do not know. I know from my own research there has been a number of targeted individual suicides. There is a program to target and kill suspected terrorist overseas using drones at a push of a button while watching a video monitor; no one would think it would happen here but if you notice there is more domestic terrorism rhetoric in the news. I also noticed the room below almost always had the curtains closed but I made on interesting observation - I saw a walkie talkie in the window. If you remember I could feel bumping below me when I was lying down and the banging or dragging of equipment above my position like there was a person above and below. The walkie talkie would have been used for communication. My time at Edgecombe Avenue was spent having the perpetrators try various new electronic harassment methods over time. I believe this is called in the targeted individual community "non consensual experimentation." There would be the foggy or blurred vision; pricked eyes or the sensation of dust in the eyes; the sensation of hearing loss; tooth pain; a pierced, singed or blistered tongue; blood in stool after being targeted in the stomach or anal region; and more recently a whiplash

sensation while targeted to the back of the neck. It seems
these people with the pain ray technology test it out in a
lab somewhere (engineering research & development
(ER&D)) and then try it on a targeted individual seeing
what's effective.

Meanwhile The Pain Ray Treatment Continued At Work

The first couple of years the pain ray harassment was
strong - not only at home but also in the workplace. At
work I was still being targeted while sitting in the lobby
with the Active Denial 'repel effect' and I believe my job
was in the process of moving to a new location because
the client the Port Authority was relocating to lower
Manhattan at 4 World Trade - I mean that in the literal
sense since the skyscraper had just been built. The initial
plan was I would go to another site and not the new
skyscraper with the client but the electrician who worked
for the client I believe knew I was getting electronic
harassed and said I should moved to the new building.
After the pain ray assaults began I wasn't treated too
kindly at my job as if there was some type of slander or
defamation. People would use terms like "anti-social"
even though I never been convicted of a crime - one
former employee said it was coming from the client - The
Port Authority. It was implied that I carried a laptop
because of nefarious activity when in fact my laptop

contained art, music, and my own UFO research. During a random inspection a security manager from the client's Chief Security Office named Carlton Cummings popped in asking about my mother (who was being targeted). He seemed somewhat alarmed that after I got directed energy assaulted at work early in the morning hours, I took a ladder from a computer server room and was inspecting the ceiling, looking above ceiling tiles to see if I could spot where a directed energy device was being concealed, at least that was my impression when shortly after he showed up looking angry. Other high ups also brought up my mother which seemed a strange way to start a conversation like a type of psychological warfare or gaslighting that is commonly reported by other targeted individuals. The PA would also express fake concern of how I felt. One interesting thing to note about this new building, and I recorded this with my laptop, is whenever the pain ray weapon was being used in the workplace like it was concealed and remotely controlled somewhere, I could hear these tiny audible clicks from the ceiling. It seemed the more stronger the activity, there was the more clicking type sounds. I even tried standing on chairs put on top of a work desk to remove ceiling tile panels and to see if I could spot anything but there were just pipes, metal shafts fluorescent light fixtures. One interesting story that is work related, while still in the old location at 225 Park Avenue South where I was situated in the lobby, a security guard only working part time would come by. His name was Mohan and claimed to do security for the

Trump family, even driving Trump family members around. This was before Donald Trump became a presidential contender. I got the impression Mohan was there to observe my harassment but it could have also been coincidence. When questioned about Trump he would say things like Trump mostly sits in his office and says dumb stuff, kind of like his now famous Twitter post or Truth social, although he also claimed the Trump family was pretty down-to-earth, and that some of what you see on TV like the reality TV show The Apprentice is just for entertainment. I asked Mohan if he was payed well and he said no. He was employed through a security contractor like I was. I later learned Trump for protection surrounds himself with former FBI. As Donald Trump became a serious presidential contender the contractors at my work site started kissing Mohan's ass, some of which I suspected knew about my targeting or were involved like the contractor at my job installing camera and security surveillance equipment. Mohan eventually quit before Trump was elected and became very patriotic wanting to join the military. A Marine Reservist who was a security guard on the executive floor, would check in for the morning roll call and taunt me making slurred speech. I got the impression because of the TBN type symptoms I was experiencing (I was targeted in the head a lot during that time and suffering from sleep deprivation and would slur some of my words). The Marine Reservist would try and talk Mohan out of joining the military thinking he was not military material. The Marine

Reservist employee was very articulate and had a way with people but also had a habit of lying. He would eventually get a job in law enforcement part of the K9 unit with no higher education. The Port Authority of New York and New Jersey had a history of ethical issues. I was there during the Bridgegate Scandal. One of the people involved in the scandal used to come in and just gave me a disgusted look. It seems government bureaucracies are a breeding ground for corruption. They value interpersonal skills but seem to lack ethical qualities and are very hierarchical in nature, releasing memos and having constant meetings over every little issue. It was funny trying to see some of them push their weight around trying to intimidate others who they view as subordinates making statements like "Do you know who I am?" especially when something happened and someone might get the blame; also the condescending nature many of them have towards a person like a security guard who is not in a favorable position. Yet the same people tend to be absent minded, leaving out details of what floor guest for a meeting is supposed to go or even getting the dates that security had to clear up. These are people who are supposed to be college educated. It points out the dangers in letting the government have no transparency in what they do, even if they play up threats like terrorism, or 9-11-01. I later learned after researching the Port Authority who had their now police department that they worked with Federal agencies like the FBI's Joint Terrorism Task Force (JTTF).

Toxic Employee/ Informant At Work

At work I had the impression that some of my co-workers
may be informants. One former co-worker made the
comment that a co-worker named Santiago could look at
my laptop and report that I was a terrorist. This employee
would bring up things that I never mentioned like UFOs
or things I would say when alone or stuff I would
communicate via E-mail with my father. Very similar to
the client asking how's my mother - the head game,
gaslighting stuff. I learned when dealing with informants
just play dumb and brush off what they say like it doesn't
bother you. Claiming someone is an informant, even
though you kind of know they are, will just make you
look paranoid. So it's an issue I never bring up nor the
electronic harassment for obvious reasons. Instead at that
time I wrote a book detailing my electronic harassment.
It's important to gather proper evidence and go about
things a certain way without discrediting yourself. I
noticed the former employee who implied Santiago was
an informant would also glance and stare at my laptop
like he was instructed to report what he saw. I believe this
was the 'insider threat' type stuff that the client was using
to get the counter-terror spending, testing out the pain ray
weaponry.

Black Bags With Skin Irritants Put in Clothes and Uniform at Work; Poison Ivy

Some targeted individuals believe nano material is used against them. Always non-lethal tactics of various degrees. I'm not sure I can attest to that but the perpetrator(s) started to put itching fibers in my clothes in my workplace locker where I kept my corporate security uniform and in my clothes at home, usually a day or two after doing my laundry. I believe someone was doing a black bag putting the itching fibers in my clothes at home. I suspect it's the same people in the building using the directed energy. Alda, the woman I'm renting a room from is probably being cooperative in letting them in. If I shook my clothes at work I could see the tiny things floating in the air. I even took some photographs using my laptop camera. A little white fiber can be made out looking like a chopped strand of hair. At work it could be any number of the Government-related client people in security management involved in the harassment campaign going through my locker. Sometimes a little bit of a rash on my and like poison ivy was rubbed on something. It fits an overall pattern of the harassment happening both at home and at work. The purpose of using non-lethal tactics like skin irritants is course psychological, to decrease one's morale. i.e. psychological warfare. Also behavioral reinforcement - the powers that be do not approve of your behavior therefore you are being punished. The people getting paid to do black bags are either an intelligence contractor or maybe the Joint Terrorism Task Force (JTFF) claiming a terrorist disruption. Someone skilled at picking locks (doors, pad locks, cars) is involved in the blackballs.

Skin Irritants - Biological or Chemical Attacks

I would get an unusually amount of colds or have flu-like symptoms or sometimes just feel like I'm coming down with a cold/ sore throat feeling. My Mom, who was targeted family on the West Coast, where it's warm and sunny most of the year would describe the same thing. Also uncontrollable sneezing where the nose feels irritated like a chemical agent was put in the air with irritation to the nostrils. Then there were times I had a runny nose out of the blue with no cold. Then there were times I had nasal burning sinus discomfort like rhinitis. The chem-attacks also happened at work when I was alone like something was put in the air.

Why I kept working the same dumb job even though it got worse?

Part of the reason I kept working the same job, at the Port Authority for Summit Security, instead of just quitting or running scared like other TI's, is I had health benefits through a Union and I knew that the government was behind the harassment. If the story broke that the government was abusing directed energy weapons (DEWs) like news of the Havana Syndrome I would have a good case against my employer and employers client - the Port authority of New York and New Jersey (PANYNJ) who always gets sued - so much so that they have their own legal department. It was also in close proximity to a junior college I went to - BMCC. There is also the other issue of those who are ostracized by society eventually becoming homeless unable to find work (terrorist watch-listed, employment blackballing). Now when I see the homeless I have a new found respect or understanding of their plight. Some of them may have been targeted by the government and driven to homelessness. How many? I'm not sure but everyone can agree there is a growing homeless problem and more people are struggling to make ends meet. I believe the countries decline is also an explanation for the electronic harassment - it's a job program for vets, growing Federal bureaucracies, intelligence contractors (PIAs). Most of these people part of the perp community are not very well educated in the humanities or liberal arts and have a gung-ho perspective on life. There's also the scarcity of well paying jobs. There's an ugly aspect to our society that can be very human exploitative, not just criminal behavior like human trafficking. America has the largest prison populations, outspends the entire world on military, and tens of thousands have been killed by the opioid crises largely fueled by the greedy pharmaceutical industry. The targeting industry is no exception, it represents a type of abuse that is occurring involving homeland security. People taking advantage of a lack of transparency to make money picking on or bullying citizens. This also explains increased alarmism by the government - to sustain this self-serving industry.

Electronic Harassed at BMCC College; Student Informants; FBI Faculty

I went to a college named Borough of Manhattan Community College (BMCC). I would take late afternoon or evening classes and then go to work during the overnights. After a class had ended there was usually a few hours of free time. As you could imagine taking college classes while getting electronic harassed was tuff. I was tired so I would sleep at the college in their recreational areas. I started to feel the pain ray. Allowing me to sleep would defeat the purpose of the electronic harassment. I tried to figure out how and where it was happening. One day I moved to another floor or different parts of the college building and noticed it was stronger in certain areas like the window. Or if I went to a certain area of a study hall it would start up there after awhile. There was one Muslim-American student named Fahid who tried to befriend me, always asking for my phone number or trying to text message. At first I just assumed he was just being friendly trying to network with other students. He was one of those students that would disrupt a class asking a lot of questions and voicing his opinion challenging the professor. He also dressed like a slob, kind of like me. Then would try to hang around with me after class and talk. Once he wanted to know where I went after class. I told him sometimes I go to Little India and eat Indian food. I made a statement about something being queer while on the train with him and he took offense like part of cancel culture/ the culture wars. I couldn't tell if it was because he was gay or being politically correct. He used to always tell me to post YouTube videos about anything that's on my mind and monetize my account. One day I got tired of him and brought up that he might be the FBI. He got mad and bought up ringing in the ear (which I never mentioned) and that the FBI might storm the area at any moments notice. He said his major was criminal justice. One day I saw him as not a slob but with another person neatly dressed in black clothes scoping out the area. He had a different calm demeanor. My last semester I never saw the guy but when I first started going to college he would pop up somewhere. I can't prove he was an informant or a TI when he mentioned ringing in the ear but he came across as an informant. One day I heard two guys who were taking computer science classes. They were outside the classroom in a seating area. An older student was talking to a younger Asian student who seemed impressionable. The older student mentioned that a professor who oversees the computers in a computer lab works for the FBI. I butted into the conversation since I was seated close by and made the comment that I thought that was creepy, the older student said he knows but the professor who works for the FBI is a good guy. Another interesting thing is some of the professor's seem to be friendly at first and then it was like they heard something bad about me and were rather off putting. I remember in my Macroeconomics class I would get targeted in the throat two weeks in a row - the sensation of gagging or having to cough. I ended up passing all my courses and earning a degree anyway. I went to the graduation ceremony at Madison Square Garden (MSG), as Senator Chuck Schumer who made an appearance spoke during the ceremony I started to get hit in the throat again. I did my best not to uncontrollably cough. Senator Chuck Schumer, of course would bring up counterterrorism in his speech. Funnily enough, I tried writing to him and Charles Rangel when the pain ray harassment began and received a form letter response. Nothing was ever done. It's been rare that any US politician has acknowledge the targeting phenomenon or tried to put a stop to it - they are in the business of pleasing big money interest.

Government agencies are no help. They are the Perps.

When living in New York I tried contacting the FCC that is mostly concerned with electronic interference from other electronic devices. The irony is if a targeted individual tried active shielding like a jamming device that interfered with other tenants electronic devices in a building they may get a visit from the FCC, not so much the perpetrators using the directed energy devices against you. Abusing emerging technology non-lethal weapons like directed energy by the authorities is also counter to upholding the US constitution or a pledge to protect public safety. The US state department investigating the Havana Syndrome that it now calls using the euphemism 'anomalous health incidents' when contacted sends back a form letter response to refer people to the FBI if you are not a state department employee. This has not worked on my end nor other TI's from what I gather. In fact there is strong indication that it may involved the Justice Department (DoJ) or what some have referred to the weaponized government. In 2023 there was an intelligence assessment by seven intelligence agencies disputing the possibility of directed energy yet it was at odds by a previous assessment with an independent panel of experts who believed "pulsed microwave attacks" was the culprit. Like most things government the intelligence assessment lacked specifics even unwilling to name the intelligence agencies involved. The Washington Post reporting the story was careful using word play not mentioning intermediate force (IFC) even though it's listed in DoD documentation citing Non-Lethal DE. I believe the vagueness and less than forthcoming nature is driven by a motivation to mature DEW proliferation and the intelligence community (IC) connection to intelligence contractors (PIAs), similar to how Russia used the Wagner Group yet was able to distance itself from the actions of the mercenaries. Suffice to say, the government is no help for TI's however it is becoming harder to outright dismiss the possibility of DEWs being abused against human targets and it will only get worse in the future with electromagnetic weapons (EW) becoming predominant in warfare. I believe the public will become more aware of the potential misuse of newer weaponry using the EMF spectrum like directed energy (DE) that can not be seen but felt.

Meanwhile Family Member Harassed In Retirement Home

My mother's problem did not end after my big sister became guardian moving her to a retirement home in Pasadena, California. She claims to have to go to sleep by a certain time or will not be able to. It seems the pain ray will start up during the evening time. I observed two perfect round red circles on each of her toes while we went to the beach. She tried keeping her feet underneath the sand thinking it would help. The perpetrator's would target her legs and feet where it was hard to walk. I think she may have been institutionalized for psychological examination in trying to complain thinking it was criminal activity. At one point it got so bad the African American lady running the retirement center at Arbor Vista in Pasadena tried to run her off by accusing her of petty stuff like clogging the drains. The past few years have been rough - she's had to use a walker to get around because of her legs being targeted. She called in middle of the night claiming to sit on the floor in trying to avoid being targeted in her bed and could feel the equipment being used like it may have been concealed or placed nearby making a vibration. The people targeting her and involved in targeting family are involved in elder abuse and violating basic human rights. On a visit to Pasadena, California while still living in New York and driving her in a rental car to look at an AirBnB room that I would be staying at - what I term the long distance directed energy could be felt in my jaw or mouth; she was in visible pain getting out of the car to look at the Airbnb. I decided it would be good to get away from the area and visit a relative living in the Yucca Valley. As we drove on Highway 210 getting further away from Pasadena and the LA area the pain ray sensation stopped. I missed my exit and was driving around Palm Springs, the site of the giant wind farm and there was no directed energy. She felt better and could walk without the aid of the walker. It seemed the directed energy was strong in the Los Angeles area but not so in more sparsely populated-desert areas. It makes me believe the long range harassment using directed energy may have to do with equipment installed where there is lots of cell phone coverage pointing to microwave antennas/ cell towers or placed on a building. More recently I observed the directed energy was more present in low population areas like when visiting my sister who lives in Joshua Tree. I also recently took some time off while living in California driving around various areas and the directed energy appeared to be stronger in more populated areas including other states like Pahrump, Nevada; Quartzsite, Arizona; and Maricopa County in Phoenix, Arizona. I also made the correlation that the targeting was strong near police stations that had large towers. While driving through the California mountains or the desert like in Death Valley I got tinnitus discomfort to the left ear where I believe a tag (TTL) was inserted deep in the ear canal that acts as a type of transponder or tracking device, while the normal electronic harassment ceased probably because the area was desolate and had poor cell coverage. It supports my theory equipment for directed energy attacks are placed around cities to guard against what the government considered 'critical infrastructure.'

Targeted While On Vacation

As you learned from my experience traveling to California, visiting my mother who is being targeted, I've also experience the pain ray treatment while on vacation. At first visiting my father in Northern Italy there was no harassment. I remember my first trip in 2014 or 2015 I slept like a baby. It actually felt weird not being hit with directed energy. Total silence, not even the tinnitus. In subsequent trips however that would all change. I remember one visit I stayed at an Airbnb rental near my father's place in an apartment building. I thought this was a great deal. Here I was in Northern Italy with an apartment all to my self at a low price. I went when it was cold, not exactly tourist season. The other catch was the heater and hot water would shut off after 20 minutes and you had to trip a switch by stepping outside the front door. Still here I was in Italy, and it seemed like a nice escape from the electronic harassment that I was getting in New York. Two or three days later the sound of children running above me and Italians talking stopped. There was dead silence by the apartment neighbors on the floor above and here came the dragging of equipment pacing my position with the sensation of the pain ray. Not only in the living room but also the bedroom. There would also be the bouncing of a ball to let me know that that the perpetrator or perpetrators were there (like I bounced a ball to taunt them in the room rental on 164th street in New York). I did not tell my father, he would get in his car and drive me to the AirBnB rental when it was getting late to be on the safe side, even though the streets seemed safe enough. I didn't want him to react in anger going up to where the perpetrators were. He would tell the story of his father if what was happening to me happened to him he would go up there and whip their ass - my Dad's father who fought in the war was not a very nice person especially when it came to being pushed around. I also knew the harassment was a type of provocation and a confrontation in a foreign country was probably not a wise decision. Before leaving I received a phone call from the AirBnB host and she seemed pretty creeped out or scared judging from her voice asking if everything is okay. It's like she heard something was going on inside the building. My last visit in October 2019, I stayed at an airbnb in a two story building near Malpensa Airport and was targeted by someone upstairs who paced my position below. I had pee all the time as my stomach was targeted and was always tired. Toward the end of my stay I caught something similar to the coronavirus, coughing up mucus and flu like symptoms. Upon returning to America there was news of the coronavirus spreading in North Italy after it was spreading in Wuhan, China. I can't say if it was related but I found it very coincidental like maybe non lethal chemical warfare gone wrong. I did observe more Chinese tourist when I was there in 2019. That would be the more likely explanation how it spread in Northern Italy just after I left.

Targeted In Hotel Rooms

Also on vacation while staying at hotels, especially when being booked in advance on my laptop, the pain ray harassment would start up. It seemed to come from a hotel room nearby. That's judging from the bumping that I would hear like someone was close-by in the adjacent room. This of course could also be explained by other hotel occupants but it seemed to coincide with the harassment. A prime example is when me and my mother (targeted family member) went to see my sister in Texas who was recovering from an automobile accident. I checked into a one-story hotel in Stephenville, Texas. My mom stayed with my sister in her trailer. I believe in this hotel the electronic harassment started right away - maybe a day later after checking in. I had booked hotel reservations far in advance - maybe that's why. This was one of those one story rectangular shaped budget hotel buildings surrounded by a parking lot. There was a family from India that was in the office and it smelled like Indian food. I asked them where I could get some Indian food but they didn't seem to understand or recommend anything. Stephenville, Texas is a college town west of Forth Worth. It has a large Walmart, BBQ and Mexican food restaurants but not really known for cuisine from southern Asia. At one point I lived in Stephenville, Texas and worked at a factory there during the late 1990s. My grandparents moved us there because my mother just could not pay the rent in Dallas on her own and I also had trouble holding down a job. Ironically, Stephenville, Texas greatest claim to fame was the 2008 Stephenville, UFO flap and in fact the relative that my mom and I were visiting had UFO sightings. I remember, we rented a small wooden house sort of close to the town square and my sister was in the backyard smoking a cigarette, she ran inside looking pale claiming to have seen a flying saucer with rotating lights slowly moving over houses. She claims a co-worker where she worked at a gas station saw the same thing. This would have been the early 2000s before I moved to an apartment in Northern Dallas or Richardson, Texas where my electronic harassment would begin. Now in the present time this electronic harassment was some type of program like from a dystopian future that was like living out a nightmare. My hotel room was a basic economy type thing with a bed, tv on a counter, and small restroom. I think the perpetrator was in the room next to mine because I could hear the sound of something solid or metallic bumping from the wall behind me, that coincided with the sensation of being hit with a pain ray. Before one jumps to the conclusion in my description of the sound of bumping at a hotel. It wasn't like people partying or fooling around - it sounded like someone using equipment. My mother claimed to also be pestered while staying with my little sister in her trailer. She was in a spare room toward the back of the trailer and the directed energy was disturbing her sleep. She tried putting an handkerchief around her head and was having a real hard time while there and wanted to leave. Meanwhile my little sister was complaining about pain, related to her automobile accident. I tried to determine where the electronic harassment was coming from. It was a typical trailer park with trailers next to each other. The neighbors next to my little sister's trailer appeared to be very private. The window curtains were never opened. I asked her who lived there and she said two men but it was hard to determine if they were involved. When we were all in my rental car I had to drop by my hotel room again and there with the door open at the room next to mine was a woman sitting outside in one of those camping looking chair's with sunglasses. It was like she wanted to pass the time being outside instead of being stuck in a hotel room like she was keeping post or something. It wasn't really an attractive looking woman either. The perpetrators to me always have a street clothes cop look, or former military, former felons who spent time in prison, even the women perpetrators. It's also important to note that Aaron Alexis, the Navy Yard shooter, also claimed to be followed to a hotel room where he was being electronic harassed. The FBI claimed he was delusional but what he described closely fits my experience be electronic harassed at hotels.

Targeted at Airbnb

During 2019-2020 I planned to quit my security guard job working at 4 World Trade. The security company I worked for Summit Security was bought out by the national chain Allied Universal. There was a dispute over rent because the woman I paid room rental rent to was always gone on vacation to the Dominican Republic and someone, probably a relative, was pocketing the cash I placed under her door each week. I moved my belongings to a public storage in the South Bronx and decided to stay at Airbnbs. I could tell the lock was picked at the public storage where itching powder was put in a bag of clothes like in my uniform at work kept in a locker. I was followed an harassed at close range moving around to various Airbnb's. In one weekly rental in Sunnyside, Queens I could tell the perps were on the floor above mine and the name of tenant had been recently removed from the call box out front. Moving around from Airbnb to Airbnb while working was also physically taxing and more expensive.

In 2020 Active Denial Resurfaced In The News During Trump's Wall; BLM Protest

In the summer of 2020 before moving to LA I took a day off from work and took a bus to Washington D.C. George

Floyd BLM protest were happening during that time and overshadowed any lone protest attempt I made but shortly afterward I learned a person at the Pentagon suggested using Active Denial (ADS) against the woke young protesters and there was the suggestion to use it at the border wall. The use of ADS never materialized but it was noted in the news. I also learned of the DE Systems Symposium that took place in Washington after I left comprising of defense contractors like Booz Allen. One of the speakers talked about directed energy intermediate force capabilities using non-lethal directed energy.

Targeted After Moving to Los Angeles (2020-2024)

After moving to Los Angeles in 2020 I purchased a used car and slept in it doing gig work like Postmates. I noticed my smartphone would often get hot and overheat as to try and disrupt my deliveries and I would be hit with directed energy prompting to try to pad my clothing to offer some type of shielding protection. When trying to lay down and sleep in the backseat I would receive the active Denial 'goodby effect' where I could feel pressure waves hitting a wider portion of my body, even creating sounds inside the car as if physical objects were affected during an attack. The Active Denial 'repel effect' would be felt while driving. The repel effect is when only one small area of the body is targeted like the head or stomach.

There would also be burning or pricking of the eyes and targeting of the mouth catching the tongue creating discomfort when I would stop and park to eat. My Mom, who is targeted family, also described continued electronic harassment, living in a retirement home in Pasadena, CA called Arbor Vista as well as a hostile living environment. She claimed her feet and legs were targeted while laying down to sleep making it hard for her to walk in the morning having to use the aid of a walker. In 2023 the targeting changed where I could detect audible pulses like BB's hitting the dashboard at intervals shortly followed by pain, usually to the stomach to try and cause incontinence, that caused frequent urination, oily and sometimes bloody stools or diarrhea depending on the severity of the targeting. After hearing the pulses my stomach could also be heard churning. This type of targeting has continued to the present day upon the writing of this book. I noticed a pattern to the targeting like a break in activity on Federal holidays and when the President was in the city. . Most think protecting the president involves the secret service but when traveling to a city it also involves state and local law enforcement personnel.

The Crying Perp Phenomenon (Remorse Syndrome)

On a visit to California which I previously mentioned where my mother was being targeted on her feat and later her legs being targeted and having to use a walker, before going to the beach we went to a grocery store nearby. A group of people maybe two or three came to stand next to us, acting a little strange. While I was getting ready to check out one short woman part of the group was staring at my mother crying. I recall this was reported by another targeted individual - like some people are unwillingly part of these programs, showing remorse or still having a conscience. This reminded me of the Milgram Experiment which was a psychological experiment to see if a person would apply electric shock to another when instructed to by an authority figure. That vacation was weird, the weather was nice, the beach was pleasant, I remember someones pet parrots where flying overhead at the beach yet I was getting microwaved and my mother, the targeted family member, was also experiencing pain. The targeted individual phenomenon is one of those contrasting things; a type of juxtaposition where it could be nice outside and very pretty, yet there is an element of oppression and cruelty hanging overhead. Sometimes the atmosphere around you isn't very nice and its pure dread; it's easy to feel down on oneself as the psychological warfare takes effect but it appears some perps may be suffering too in knowing right from wrong. Los Angeles does remind me of the horror movie Night of The Living Dead. It's a weird place where people walk around like zombies having pure apathy toward one another. New

York City on the other hand is a sanitized world for the affluent who's number one leisure activity is walking their dog. People have more compassion for their pet than their fellow man, it seems judging by the condition you see some homeless people are in. It's that marginalized and ostracized segment of society. Targeted individuals also fit into this world of exclusion - people who are being picked on, bullied, pestered by those serving the establishment trying to justify spending on perceived threats

Targeted While Flying (Where's The Air Marshal! - He's a Terrorist)

While going to visit relatives or on vacation the pain ray could be felt on passenger jets. In recent years it has gotten worse not only to fly but the severity of the electronic harassment on planes. I used to wonder how it was possible, thinking of some targeted individuals who believe satellites are being used. I've always been skeptical of the satellite claim due to the distance a signal would have to travel, the logistics involved etc. I remember seeing a web site claiming Iridium satellites were involved. I knew though based on my own experience the stronger directed energy assaults involved people using equipment at close range. I remember when it was just ringing in the ear, enough to be uncomfortable.

In recent years parts of the body has been targeted with the stronger pain ray harassment. I took a plane flight to Miami which was delayed for five hours at Laguardia Airport - I was taking advantage of an airline voucher from a previous canceled flight. As the airline finally departed I felt being targeted hard in the chest and sometimes in the throat with the uncontrollable urge to cough, once the plane achieved high altitude. Likewise my most recent trip to Pasadena, California there was targeting in the heart or chest area. It felt I may have a heart attack but I just took the pain in stride, even though there is a little fear that those abusing directed energy technology may get carried away and you may go into cardiac arrest. I think the dilemma with passenger aircraft pose to the perpetrators is the whole motive of the electronic harassment is to cause sleep deprivation. A person on a long flight, un-pestered can get a good nights sleep or a nice long nap. It's also an excuse for more spending and testing the technology on airliners. It also points to who is really behind the program due to TSA screenings, luggage x-rayed before boarding a flight - there has to be government involvement. It seemed the harassers wanted to up the ante. After all they had free rein testing and using the less-than lethal technology on people with little or no accountability or public scrutiny. What abusive people don't understand though, is after awhile the abused person stops caring because it's not much of a life anyway. This is one of the flaws of pain reinforcement or applying more physical abuse to achieve and objective - it can only be so effective before a person becomes desensitized. So called game-changing less-than lethal technology also has limitations - it may not avert tragedy if the so-called terrorist being targeted knows its only intended to inflict pain or just to scare someone. I was targeted heavily in the chest/heart while going to California from New York. On the return flight home however something strange happened. The plane was delayed on the return. I forget if it was a mechanical issue or due to traffic but I felt that something was afoot. After boarding the plane a strange man sat by me who seemed void of emotion. I had a window seat and as the plane reached high altitude I could feel the pain ray hitting my chest. At one point I left my seat excusing myself to go to the restroom. A creepy woman sitting a few seats back had out a tablet as if she was watching something. As I passed by her seat and stared at her and the device she had in her hand, it was as if she did not notice me coming and was taken aback, quickly concealing whatever she was looking at and bending downward toward her legs. I thought her behavior was rather peculiar. As the plane landed at JFK Airport, everyone started to exit but I stayed-put observing. The strange man seated next to me didn't understand why I was not getting up to leave and slowly left himself. I got the impression he was extra-security in case the directed energy assault made me act out. Sure enough the woman who I caught off guard earlier that was looking at a device, stayed behind too and was the last one to get off the plane who was with a man who appeared to have a brace on his leg and was using crutches. I thought to myself it looks suspect - he didn't seem that injured. The woman at this point proceeded to take down some rather heavy overhead luggage and had trouble pulling it down the airplane isle as they both proceeded to exit. A flight attendant standing behind them looked visibly upset seeing me watch them as I was the last one to get off the plane. I overheard her making a comment that the plane should have had a sky marshal onboard while conversing with other flight attendants glancing in my direction. I thought to myself, am I really that scary looking or just made out to be this bad person? I followed the man with what looked like a fake injury walking along with his crutches and the woman continue to struggle with her very heavy luggage-case, pulling it down the bridge tunnel that connects the plane to the terminal. After exiting the plane they stopped at a restroom nearby talking to each other showing concern when noticing me trailing. I continued to walk past a bit and then sat in a chair where boarding passengers were waiting for a departure. After they exited the restroom I followed behind. A man stopped in his tracks standing behind me and had an expression of shock and concern. He came across as a look-out man. I had my iPhone out pretending to take video of the woman with her heavy luggage and the man with crutches and they appeared to be on edge, then I turned the phone toward the look-out man and he quickly turned around not wanting to be filmed. The woman with the heavy luggage and man with crutches of course were not taking the public transport - they probably had a car waiting at tax payer expense. I just kind of laughed it off and proceeded to walk toward the AirTrain to catch the New York subway like all the other lower class mortals/ potential terrorist being picked on by big brother. I knew from that point though how the directed energy assaults were occurring when I was flying on a passenger aircraft. I thought of an article published in New Scientist from 2008 where it described the National Institute of Justice (NIJ) developing prototypes of portable (mmWave) pain ray equipment with a limited range - not the Active Denial but something even smaller that would fit inside a suitcase.

Targeted Individual Groups and Controlled Opposition or FBI Shills

I attended a very small scale TI protest in 2015 and by 2017 to 2019 there were larger efforts to protest by targeted individual support groups and organizations, not only here in the US where some of the bigger protest took place in cities like Chicago, Sacramento but also internationally like Poland, Japan, Korea yet these protest have garnished little to no media coverage. My efforts to report directed energy abuse to both local and national media went ignored, instead what occurred later is dismissive articles that now appear atop of Google search results when using the search term 'targeted individuals.' It's strange to see 20 to 50 people walking around holding up signs in broad daylight out of desperation over targeting and it not being reported. I got the impression some of these TI groups were really just controlled opposition using pseudo-terminology like 'organized stalking' with a fake video blogger walking around saying the Mandela Effect. Another tactic was using an agent provocateur screaming conspiracies like the Masons are behind it. One organization that formed after I attended the 2017 Unity and Hope conference in Boston tried to be overly conspiratorial like Infowars with a boiler print web site making unsubstantiated rumors and claims using conspiratorial diagrams. There was a falling out amongst members resulting in a lawsuit where the real identity of some of the members were revealed who were going under a pseudonym. Before a protest there appeared to be some in-fighting amongst targeted individual personalities and targeted individual groups online as if to try and disrupt any real mobilization. A TI organization in the US (not mentioning names) had a notorious reputation, with former members alleging a misappropriation of funds by the leader and the organization having to change its name. Some suspect that these groups are just front organizations by the intelligence community used for containment so there is no real mobilization or designed to gathering info - keeping tabs on TI's. There have been numerous survey's, request that personal info be given for a class action lawsuit against the government yet nothing really materializes - the government also has sovereign immunity. One survey was by some former NSA whistle blowers, the name William Binney comes to mind, yet nothing came out of it. I appeared on a call-in support group show called Ella Free after attending the 2017 Unity and Hope conference in Boston (a TI convention) because I was recommended to appear by one of the attendees. I never contacted the call-in show host, partly due to her anonymous nature using a pseudonym which I found suspect. I received a call out-of-the-blue from the host, because I handed out my phone number at the conference. The host tone was rather off-putting like I was reluctantly being invited as a guest. I gave a rather awkward interview, partly due to my environment - when the interview took place I was at college, and the fact I had a cheap pre-paid phone that was hard to hear. I later became suspicious, not only because the call in-host kept her identity anonymous but from also listening to the show's archives - some of the call-ins appeared to be staged with frequent interruptions like samples were being triggered. Other times people would be interrupted when giving interesting testimony and things would go off on a tangent - other callers talking over each other and so on. That said my interview that I gave back in 2017 is available on Soundcloud and Internet Archive and is for the record. When the coronavirus hit it ended targeted individual protest efforts and also during that time there was greater online censorship, a conspiracy theory crack down, and shadow banning. After researching private intelligence (PIAs) and news of Harvey Weinstein and Black Cube I learned about fake online accounts called sock puppets, avatar operators, and that the FBI helped law enforcement to create 'alias identities' in order to monitor people on social media. I knew the FBI tries to infiltrate groups and activist and I'm sure targeted individual activist efforts where nothing substantial materialized was no exception. It was reported that the FBI intimidated Occupy Wall Street protesters to help end the movement with a knock on the door where the protesters lived - it seems rather undemocratic, a violation of the First Amendment.

Targeted Individual Protest, Controlled Opposition, and Retaliation (Another Violation of the US Constitution)

In the years 2015-2017 I attempted to protest electronic harassment and the the covert harassment use of directed energy that resulted in relation with stronger attacks.

09-15-2015. Targeted Individuals - Time To Fight. White House Protest. The Revolution Has Begun

I met Todd Griffen from Oregon who was staying in Washington D.C. and two other TI's from North Carolina. We stood in front of the White House holding crude signs I made using a marker. Todd Griffen who claimed to be abused at the Organ State Hospital and a proponent of conspiracy author Dr. Robert Duncan had his own sign and recorded a live feed using the Periscope App. One of the TI's from North Carolina said my targeting was ultrasonic (USW) after describing the modulating tone I heard using a piezo mic and that is was from a resonator. Todd said there was a larger TI protest in Washington some weeks prior to our protest with a TI activist named Tyrone Dew, also a man at that protest became very agitated was arrested and involuntary committed by cops. Active shooters Aaron Alexis (2013) and Myron May (2014) who made statements about electronic harassment before snapping resonated with some TI's like Tyrone Dew.

2015-2016. Lone Protest in New York City

I tried protesting in front of the Federal Building in Lower Manhattan and was run off by a DHS police officer and I tried protesting a number of times at the United Nations building in Manhattan handing out photocopies and holding a sign. One other person showed up named Messiah Santiago from the Bronx. He saw an add I posted on a street post in Times Square. At first I thought he was an agent provocateur because he was loud and yelling. He claimed E-Mail hacking and the government under Obama killed his father. He was a champion of Donald Trump while Trump screaming his name to UN employees. This was when Trump first started running for President.

October 2017. Unity and Hope Conference in Boston, MA.

A conference that had about 20 or 30 TI's from around the US. It had TI Internet personalities giving powerpoint presentations and some by video. The Havana Syndrome made the news during the summer and was the talk of the conference. The organizer claimed to suffer from V2K and was in the red from throwing the event. A woman there was taking a survey for NSA whistleblowers William Binney and J. Kirk Wilber but said it was closed to new submissions. I got the impression some of the people there were not really TI's, using pseudonyms instead of their real identity. A TI spoke at the event later claimed threats were made against him and his family and that many of the online TI personalities and a TI organization at the event were controlled opposition. An agent provocateur walked around outside yelling the Mason's (freemasonry conspiracy). A freelance writer for

WIRED magazine covered the event and seemed detached like she already knew what article to write, sure enough a negative article was published afterward implying delusions. A lawsuit resulted from a TI organization formed by some of the people at Unity and Hope using pseudonyms, it was alleged FBI collusion to discredit TI's by another attendee who joined their organization revealing the names of the people using pseudonyms trying to discredit TI's using conspiracies, insinuating violence against peace offices so TI's get thrown in jail. Don't fall for this fake TI organization.

2018-2019. Targeted Individual Day and Spring Day Rally

These were supposed to be annual events by TI organizations. Some of the bigger rallies were in Chicago and Sacramento holding signs that read "organized stalking." The vague term was an idea by one TI groups, it reminded me of the governments use of euphemisms. There was in-fighting online by TI's before an event like to discourage attendance. A video blogger would cover the larger gatherings repeating the words "Mandela Effect." Some international groups protested in conjunction with the event in countries like Poland and Japan in larger numbers holding banners. I briefly attended a small rally of four to five people at New York

City Hall park. I got the impression it was fake, flyers handed out had conspiracy diagrams that looked like a marginalization effort so I left.

2020. Protest efforts ceased because of the coronavirus and internet censorship (shadow banning).

2020. I called into a NY Targeted Individual support group hosted by Janey Wilson that I saw on meetup.com and received heavy electronic harassment afterward. The talk at the time was about 'Cyber-Torture.' I got the impression call in-support groups are monitored and only offered moral support for tortured souls.

2020. My Lone Protest in Washington D.C.

Before quitting my job in New York and moving to LA I tried to stage a lone protest in Washington D.C. but was drowned out by George Floyd 'BLM' protesters. I could see how the country had changed since I attended a small TI gathering to protest in 2015. Our small group stood in front of the White House gate for a photo op. In 2020 that was no longer possible because of the culture wars creating civil unrest and the extra security precautions. It was also harder to mobilize with all the sock puppets on social media and what came to be known as shadow banning (online censorship). After I left the protest I learned someone at the Pentagon proposed to use Active Denial (ADS) against protesters and a month later there was the Directed Energy Symposium. One of the speakers talked about less-than lethal directed energy and intermediate force capabilities (DE IFC). The Directed Energy Symposium speaking about the use of directed energy for intermediate force was closer to my own targeting and what could be behind the Havana Syndrome, more so than the TI protest efforts that were either controlled opposition or confused TI's embracing conspiracy authors.

Poor Journalism - No More Fifth Estate

In 2017 there were one-off articles by mainstream media publications that depicted targeted individuals as having techno phobias, delusional, and the articles often relying on a mental health expert. These articles also asserted the technology reported by TI's is science fiction. There were also articles attempting to debunk the Havana Syndrome. It was initially speculated as a sonic weapon or the 'Cuba sonic attacks' and then there were media debunking efforts like crickets, mass delusions, a byproduct of spy surveillance equipment like the Moscow Signal and then' pulsed microwave attacks' by by an independent study. The State Department under Biden decided to take the Havana Syndrome more seriously due to increased reports occurring around the world so created the euphemism 'anomalous health effects (AHIs).' After some time passed seven intelligence agencies that wanted to stay anonymous released a report trying to sweep it under the rug.

My personal opinion based on the evolution of my own targeting is it's directed energy intermediate force capabilities. (DE IFC). There's a desire to further matured DE capabilities and that explains the debunking efforts and the governments less-than forthcoming attitude creating an euphemism and trying to avoid the term directed energy (DEWs) or electromagnetic warfare (EW). There was no correlation with watch-listing, surveillance abuse, the kill list or The Disposition Matrix, intelligence contracting (PIAs) that boomed after 9-11-01. In the past the mainstream media was called the Fifth Estate to keep an overbearing government in check, like the Watergate scandal, or even the Intelligence Community (IC) revealing the FBI's COINTELPRO but many now see the media as state-sponsored propaganda.

The Reality of EMF devices and weapons - Not Science Fiction

So far in this book I covered Active Denial (ADS) technology that uses mmWave or sonic weapons like LRAD but there was research into microwave hearing weaponry like the VOICE of GOD weapon or MEDUSA that can cause Voice To Skull (V2K) which is a term that came from the military. I'm sure these programs that were canceled could have continued on out of the public's eye. It's not only that but there are many cosmetic and therapeutic devices using lasers, light, RF, and ultrasonic waves. I went to see a Dermatologist in New York for radio frequency mole removal. After the treatment a scab developed and whiting effect to the skin afterward with no scar. To imply the technology reported by TI's is science fiction is pretty asinine by the media like there is no effort put into research or people are being intentionally mislead.

The Plausible Deniability Factor of Electromagnetic Weapons (EW)

The appeal of using directed energy weapons against people is obvious. You see this with people pointing lasers like a dazzler at airline pilots - something that can get a person in trouble but it still happens. Unlike guns or conventional weaponry directed energy (DE) makes no sound and can be used remotely. Directed energy weapons (DEWs) are termed "the silent weapon." Most directed energy weapons (DEWs) are associated with military applications like high energy lasers. A short synopsis of the history of directed energy weapons is the military experimented with chemical/gas lasers that can be very powerful - think Co2 laser cutting machines or Ronald Raegan's SDI Star Wars missile defense program using weaponized satellites to shoot powerful beams at nuclear warheads, then in the early part of the 21st century the trend of directed energy started moving toward solid state technology because it is smaller, more compact than the big cumbersome chemical lasers. Many targeted individuals refer to directed energy (DE) as the less-than lethal variety or the abuse of non-lethal weapons. Directed energy as a less-lethal weapon would have appeal because of the plausible deniability factor. A conductive energy device like a taser used by law enforcement spurs a lot of controversy. It's very apparent that a non-lethal weapon is being used to try and subdue an unruly suspect because a taser has to make contact with the skin in order to emit a painful jolt of electricity. Directed energy like Raytheon's pain ray weapon can be remotely be aimed at someone. Only the target would feel the painful effects. First this technology developed by Raytheon was a big truck mounted unit powered by a Gyrotron. The Initial purpose was it would be used as a crowd control device like to help disperse an unruly mob or quell a riot. Similar to the LRAD that emits loud audio to disperse crowds. Then Raytheon developed the Silent Guardian derived from the term the silent weapon. This was smaller but still large in size. Around 2007 Wired Magazine started publishing articles that there was a desire to create smaller, more compact pain rays using solid state technology and this was being developed by Sandia National Labs; The National Institute of Justice; Raytheon. The idea was to put smaller, more compact pain ray weapon technology in the hands of law enforcement. In a New Scientist article from 24 December 2008 it claimed that a portable table top device by the NIJ was developed with the range of less-than a meter and a backpack sized prototype of 15 meters. Mysteriously, talk of smaller pain ray weaponry all but disappeared and fails to be reported by the media. In all likelihood it probably went underground. This has to do with the fear factor radiation weapons have on the public, even if it is non-ionizing radiation like Radio Frequency. So then I believe the plan by those developing and using such technology was to use it out of the public's eye on selected targets just do to the flak something like the pain ray weapon would receive. Plausible deniability and marginalization could be used to brush off a target's claims.

Family In Denial; Institutional Abuse

My big sister a proponent of mental health was set in her thinking and refused to believe directed energy was being abused. Even with my Mom needing to see a doctor because of the pain inflicted. My Dad, at first alarmed, putting away his iPad, became comfortable with denial, and rationalized it with some 'saving the world' self-righteous ideology. It shows people, even close to you can get comfortable with others being tortured, like the abuse tolerated in institutions, where it becomes normal, and there's less apathy and concern to immoral behavior, where negative assumption is directed toward the victim making the abuse okay. This was exemplified with my Mother (targeted family) being abused in a retirement home and over time she became the bad person while the people working there seemed less concerned with unethical behavior like elder abuse. It was the case at government institution like the Port Authority of New York and New Jersey (PANYNJ), it even created a more toxic work environment. Another institution where abuse is tolerated is the Pentagon. I.e. war crimes, Abuse Grahib, America's torture physchologist. This happens in may countries where institutions of authority justify torture; war crimes which is a precursor to genocide; ethnic cleansing.

The Rise of Neo-Liberal Private Intelligence Contracting (PIAs) That Correlates With the TI Phenom

I would later learn from researching targeted individuals that what is termed "threat mitigation" is now big business with the defense-intelligence industry and is probably connected to the whole targeting phenomenon as well as the Pentagon's sudden interest in UFO's (UAP). UFOs are just something else to be alarmed about i.e. why I'm targeted. I can only think of one book describing the Neo-liberal private intelligence industry (PIAs) and the occasional news headlines by the likes of Palantir & ICE, Harvey Weinstein & Black Cube etc. It's an industry that would rather stay hidden from the general public that started to receive some unwanted notoriety. Black Cube for example was an Israeli firm that Harvey Weinstein used to keep tabs on his alleged sexual harassment victims including psychological profiles on them. CBS 60 Minutes did a report on another Israeli firm named NSO Group that developed cell-phone cracking software that can be used on encrypted phones; the clients are law enforcement and intelligence agencies. Palantir a CIA backed big data company by Peter Thiel, the Billionaire co-founder of PayPal, is so secretive that is uses a SCI (Sensitive Compartmented Information) facility and not an office complex, the company works with both law enforcement on predictive policing and Federal government on data mining/database sharing - and most recently the controversy about working with ICE agents. It has also been reported that Palantir tracks so called "subversives," potential terrorist etc. I guess everyone has the makings of the potential terrorist especially if you're not rich with government connections (The government can not be considered terrorist even if they harass, a victim would be considered anti-government). Some targeted individuals will use terms like private security but these people are not companies that provide security guards to observe and report suspicious activity or deter intrusions but its comprised of people who were formally in government, defense, and intelligence. It's very similar to the mercenary (private military) business like Erik Prince's Blackwater and how that industry blossomed after 9-11-01 but instead of filling the role of the military they do jobs an intelligence agency would have traditionally done like spy work (tradecraft). I've seen some targeted individuals on the internet allege that surveillance role players (SRVs) are the actual perpetrators by defense/intelligence contractors. Looking at the employment classifieds for surveillance role player jobs some of the qualifications listed are "knowledge of surveillance tradecraft, surveillance detection techniques and terminology" and some of these jobs require a security clearance with a preference toward former military/law enforcement. There are many private intelligence contractors advertising a wide range of services from "insider threats" or whistle blowing to counter-intelligence to tackling criminal activity or the criminal element. One private intelligence company named Prescient Edge Corp. list directed energy sub systems as part of its ER&D repertoire. Mother Jones reported that since 9-11-01 private intelligence has become a lucrative business calling it the private-intelligence boom that pays more than the government counter-part. The article from Mother Jones (2013) is a decade old. I'm sure the PIA industry is bigger now. The salary on average of a private intelligence contractor is almost twice as much as the salary of a federal employee. A person will work for the FBI to get a pension then do similar work in the private sector landing contracts. Security operations were centralized at the Port Authority of New York and New Jersey (PANYNJ) that I was stationed at working as security patrol guard by The Chertoff Group. This was shortly before the pain ray (Active Denial) treatment began both at home and in the workplace. The Chertoff Group has a white paper on "insider threats" and boast about the DHS Safety Act which is limited liability protection to contractors testing counter-terror technologies. The Chertoff Group also has former CIA Director Michael Hayden as part of its team, who was criticized by the press for not being truthful on the CIA's role in torture during the Bush Presidency. Out of curiosity, I submitted an FOIA request researching my name referencing the FBI and also conducted a criminal background check by going to the police department, 1 Police Plaza, in Manhattan, New York to take finger prints and request a criminal record. Here is a free man with no criminal convictions having to get his own finger prints to try and find out why he's the victim of physical abuse by those who are supposed to serve and protect the public but really serve the state - the results came back and I had no criminal record. The FOIA request to the FBI yielded nothing - much like a written report I submitted to them in 2014 detailing what I deemed as suspect activity and being hit with directed energy - no response. I wasn't on the sex offender list so some of these PIAs targeting sex traffickers could not target me of doing that. I was not selling drugs on the dark web or part of come cartel. Now if a private intelligence agency is doing the dirty work using directed energy devices against citizens then of course and FOIA request to a Federal agency will turn up nothing. The use of contractors is one way to skirt around people's rights. The target will incriminate themselves or get themselves into trouble by trying to retaliate. Think of it as a type of retaliation or provocation. Realize if you are being targeted the purpose is probably more than inflicting pain, extrajudicial punishment but by people who claimed they worked within the law to get you out of society. In Los Angeles I realized there is a law enforcement component, threatening a cop or the sheriff is considered a terrorist act. At one of the police precincts in Manhattan a cop sad, "it isn't us doing it" but they know if you've beeb placed on the terrorist watch-list through the terrorist screening center (TSC) by the Justice Department. Recently CACI lost an effort to dismiss a lawsuit by former Abu Grahib prisoners suing under the Alien Tort Act. The prisoners blamed contractors like CACI who were part of Abu

Grahib. Some TI's protesting their targeting on Targeted Individual Day held signs that exclaimed contracted stalking. Aside from Harvey Weinstein and Black Cube or Spyware NSO Group or Palantir and ICE, America's mainstream media has done little to investigative America's private intelligence (PIA) contracting spook world even though there is a clear track record of abuse. An ethical question to ask if do we really need to with hunt, become headhunters, or lynch citizens using law enforcement and private contractors? Does that make the country more safe? Society has gotten worse and technology has been dehumanizing. The government will argue intelligence outsourcing is necessary. That may be true to an extent but such an industry like a corporation driven by profit can justify abuse where there is little accountability. Neo-liberalism is not always better. I had a college professor who pointed out the perils in Neo-liberalism and that social welfare programs "Neo-liberal stigma" was not better for the poor. If my abuse was conducted by a government agency that had to be transparent, like how the Pentagon's AATIP was revealed by FOIA, then the public would not stand for it. Edward Snowden, considered and insider threat by PIAs, is another example. He worked for a contractor Booz Allen, if it was the government maybe there could have protocols and avenues he could go through to whistle blow on surveillance abuse that infringed on civil liberties, intelligence community (IC) reforms could be enacted like a modern day Church Committee.

Computer Interference and Smart Phone Overheating A Common Occurrence

My laptop which is a MacBook would get hot like a toaster oven especially if I was involved in UFO research, self-published UFO books, or targeted individual activism like there is a cyber-warfare component to my targeting. Even though my self published graphic illustrated books were an amateur operation and not that popular and neither were my Geocities or Angelfire web sites compiling UFO info, it was made out to be a big threat by someone (most likely the Pentagon, government alarmist) and every little thing would have to be monitored. This also happened when I wasn't even on the internet like computers restarting. It was obvious and not a subtle thing. Most of the time my laptop would be normal and then the battery would quickly drain as you could hear it revving up and getting hot. Sometimes denial-of-service (DoS) attacks when using free Wi-Fi. I took my older MacBook to a repair shop and they said the problem was not the battery but something installed like spyware. Apple computers are not really known to have viruses. I purchased a new MacBook and the same issues started occurring. Sometimes the MacBook would restart by itself or I would be given an error message when trying to save a file and have to restart. It should be pointed out that the suspect activity was strong when dealing with UFOs and not so much my music projects. The funny thing is I'm not a person who uses Tor/the dark web or online encryption because I have nothing to hide. All my research whether it be UFOs or electronic harassment came from a public source and posted or published for all to see. Unlike the alarmist deceptive government, or wasteful spending Department of Defense - I have nothing to hide; no ulterior motives. No wasteful spending since I can't print money and be trillions in national debt. So it was just another example of the passive aggressive bully behavior infringing on a person's rights which tends to happen when people don't hold the government accountable and let them do anything they want with no consequences. It's not an if or when like terrorism but a given that government if given the opportunity will abuse power. Researching private intelligence (PIAs) many of these contractors operate in the cyber-world, like I saw Raytheon purchased Blackbird Technologies that specialized in hacking without a trace.

Targeted Individual Pseudo Vocabulary and Conspiracy Authors

Many TI's use their own vocabulary much like the DoD has tradecraft terminology and acronyms like CI/HUMINT or SIGINT or rabbit (for target) or SAPs

(Special Access Programs) or Intermediate Force Capabilities (IFC), using non-lethal directed energy is Directed Energy Intermediate Force Capabilities (DE IFC) or TTL (Technology Tagging, Tracking, Locating). Many targeted individuals (TI's) are not aware of the methods and terminology behind their targeting have created pseudo-terms that have become popular within the TI community like gang stalking, street theater, V2K, satellite harassment, electronic harassment, nano bots, non-consensual experimentation, spiritual warfare, neural programing, cyber-torture. They've also gravitated toward popular conspiracy authors that boast impressive credentials like a confidence trickster that write about mind control, HAARP. One the other hand the government favors the use euphemisms like anomalous heath effects in an effort not to use the word directed energy (DE) or electronic warfare (EW), also enemy combatants, extraordinary rendition to the country's role in torture diminish torture and the killing of human beings. Just because a TI uses pseudo terms like 'gang stalking' that has been used to cast doubt on TI's by the media does not mean their targeting is not happening. The fact is emerging technology like directed energy (DE) can be abused against human targets (rabbits) just as the government lied about surveillance (PRISM;TIA;"Basektball") and human experimentation in the past. Pseudo vocabulary although not deemed credible may not mean the abuse is not occurring. It could represent a cultural reaction to foul play that is really a happening. Gang stalking has often been discredited as delusional but there are examples of a coordinated effort by groups to stalk a target (rabbit). Surveillance role players (SRPs) in role playing exercises and FBI Special Surveillance Group (SSG) 'ghost.' The military did experiment with what is termed V2K or voice-to-skull. Such research could have been furthered under a different guise out of secrecy and further developed much like my own electronic harassment described in this book.

What can be legally done about Electronic Harassment?

The following is not legal advice but legal strategies to consider part of my own on-going legal research. How you plan to approach your targeting legally is under your own discretion. I know it can be daunting especially if you are being targeted by the government and can't afford a lawyer. We live in a two-tier justice system and the poor are at a disadvantage and many who are targeted are in a vulnerable position. When it comes to targeting gathering evidence is crucial. Due to the stealth nature of the non-lethal weaponry it is hard for the victim to prove abuse. Most if not all Americans don't use technical (high-band meter and probe) equipment to measure millimeter waves in the Active Denial range or would not know how to go about detecting a sonic weapon. It's much easier with conventional non-lethal weapons where the abuse involves human to human contact like a taser where there have been civil rights lawsuits against law enforcement, as well as police beatings. FOIA documents can be redacted where black bars are put through information deemed sensitive. The use of Neo-liberalism like what some targeted people term contracted stalking can make a government agency like the DoJ or FBI use plausible deniability. I believe the rise of "threat mitigation" intelligence contractors (PIAs) or what some term in conspiratorial terms "the deep state" coincides with the targeted individual phenomenon. An argument can be made that his unregulated industry lacking proper oversight is overzealous. Many in government, including politicians, believe they have liability protections like sovereign immunity. There are also liability protections passed after the Patriot Act for homeland security contractors called the DHS Safety Act but there is also "piercing the veil" and sovereign immunity may not protect those in government knowingly doing wrong like torture. Elected officials are no strangers to abuse of power or wrong doing. I also have reason to believe those involved in the actual targeting are able to hold a security clearance and operate under the oath of secrecy where there are strict penalties if they talk. All this said, I believe what constitutes as torture and physical abuse is wrong like flogging a citizen with no trial, even if they are terrorist-watch listed, and would not pass the smell test in the eyes of the public who elect the government. I also believe like MKULTRA and human experimentation that occurred in the past the covert abuse of non-lethal directed energy (DEWs) that's considered emerging weapons technology in this era will be known to the public who eventually catch on to things happening out of the public's eye. One thing a person being targeted can do is study law. Ask yourself what laws are being broken or violations do you think are occurring. For example, I experience directed energy attacks (NWL DEW's) while in the car driving and working. This could be a violation of public safety by law enforcement of they are involved. It's also depriving of rights under color of law and a violation of due process law since I also work while driving. A targeted family member is elderly and this would be considered elder abuse. I believe I was targeted over open source UFO research which would be a violation of my civil liberties. Many people are intimidated by law or frightened by the term lawsuit by seeking a legal remedy to a wrong but I believe that someone who is both tactful and articulate in a court of law can have success. Legal success has not been on the targeted individual's side and representing yourself without the use of an attorney is usually not recommended but this does not mean that a person being targeted can not become a lawyer themselves or even become more competent than some attorneys with education and experience, even if you don't pass the law exam - if the chips are stacked against you. One has to be careful about what can be considered frivolous lawsuits and developing that sort of reputation with the courts but a legal option should not be considered a lost cause either. Journalist have gotten records revealing Information about directed energy programs or other things kept secret using Federal Sunshine Laws and the FOIA. A jury trial may be a better option than a judge since a jury can be swayed. Your evidence may not be in the highest technical degree due to a lack of specialized equipment but you may have enough circumstantial evidence to convince a jury of wrong doing like in my case where I compiled evidence using low-tech methods and also researched directed energy. I observed even though DEWs are considered the "silent weapon" they still affect physical objects like a thin sheet of mylar or balloons where there is sound and movement. Never underestimate human ingenuity even if you are at a technological disadvantage. Using conspiracy theory like popular conspiracy authors embraced by some TI's may not be a good idea since "mind control" conspiracies or "pseudo-terms (gang-staling, remote neural monitoring)" that TI's use may not be viewed as credible evidence and reinforce those who will try to debunk your claims using a mental health explanation. Understand the language that the military or intelligence community uses. I.e. electromagnetic warfare (EW), intermediate force (IFC) et al. In law what can support a plaintiffs argument is a legal precedent. Former prisoners part of the Abu Grahib scandal brought a lawsuit against a contractor named CACI that was involved using the alien tort act. The alien tort act may not be an option for you since you are a citizen but highlighting similar abusive behavior brought forward in a lawsuit can support your case. Another example: Former Gitmo prisoners who claimed to be tortured were awarded financial compensation by countries outside the US. Some TI's mention class action lawsuits brought against the government but I would be weary of TI organizations bringing forward such a legal tactic who don't seem credible and overly conspiratorial trying to be Alex Jones. Can you site examples where a class action lawsuit against big brother has been successful? What about corporations or defense contractors? Due your homework and due diligence before going along with such schemes. Many TI's are isolated and the FBI has been known to infiltrate activist organizations and groups thwarting any momentum or using discrediting efforts through politics of association. I observed attending a 2017 targeted individual gathering called Unity and Hope that there appeared to be controlled opposition - people using pseudonyms who did not seem genuine. Anarchist have been known to use horizontal rule where there is a common cause and direct action but no leader. Many lawsuits by individual TI's who have a common cause may be harder to discredit and more noticeable if many are alleging the abuse of stealth weapons like directed energy (DEWs) where a lawsuit becomes part of public records.

A Push For Police Technology Transparency After 9-11 But Not Enough

Recently there has been a new push for transparency even though people in government and militarized law enforcement are still very alarmist bringing up 9-11. The police increasingly look like the military and there is lots of controversy over technology how personal data is being used for exploitative purposes, Cambridge Analytica being a prime example. Or a data mining company called Palantir using Amazon.com to help Federal Agencies like ICE track immigrants and also claimed to help the government keep track of 'subversives.' There's Palantir Gotham for predictive policing and helping cops see everything about a person before being stopped. Part of this push for transparency has a lot to do with the erosion of civil liberties and the decline of the middle class where there's a two-tier justice system. Also the rise of people with power, money, and influence wield the upper hand when it comes to technology and how it can be used against the average citizen, to exploit personal info and spy on a citizen, and to track citizens or non-citizens. Some during the coronavirus embraced vaccine conspiracies involving Bill Gates which is emblematic over people's distrust over big-tech and Microsoft developed facial recognition software for police to identify pedestrians without asking for ID where there was push back. With terms like predictive policing, the police influence in neighborhoods using community policing, being privy to watch listing, a person can make a good case that the police are actually cheating when it boast about lower crime numbers. In 2017 some New York City council members proposed the POST Act or the Public Oversight of Surveillance Technology Act. The NYPD went on the offensive arguing that revealing such technology would inhibit counter-terrorism efforts. Other cities have pushed for similar transparency. I think the main concern by those pushing for transparency was more over the controversy regarding immigration. Federal agencies such as ICE or law enforcement could easily use this technological advantage to track or snoop on people here illegally. There was also the issue of racial profiling or what is called ethnic mapping. The NYPD and CIA had a special relationship after 9-11. For example, Larry Sanchez from the CIA joined the reigns of the NYPD and would follow and stalk Muslims in New York. Of course, over time Muslims became less of a perceived threat so you hear more about domestic terrorism or homegrown terrorist. Some say the term terrorism is political. Antifa were holding up signs that White Nationalist or the KKK are terrorist and Trump was calling Antifa lefty terrorist. Then some politicians were calling active shooters terrorist after some recently well publicized cases when they may have been bullied loners or disgruntled employees (going postal). It used to be simple, the radicalized Muslim that hi-jacks planes was a terrorist but now anybody can be called a terrorist. This alarming trend of using scapegoats in politics has pushed for more transparency, not so much concerns of where all the counterterrorism spending is going, not so much our privacy or rights being violated. For a long time people gave the government a free pass on things like government snooping and data collection but now there is more concern because of contentious government policies and more and more laws being passed restricting free will. I got the impression that my own targeting is part of overbearing surveillance where everyone is watched. I.e. the Pentagon's Total Information Awareness (TIA). Even after TIA was canceled and the revelation of PRISM became known it was said such 'monitor everyone and everything' has continued under a different guise. I'm sure there are some people out there that operate with total autonomy like an off-grid isolationist dweller or traveling hobo without a phone but it antonym these days is such a rare thing. Even homeless and vagrants are tracked though the welfare-industrial complex.

The Dystopian Internet-of Things

When I researched UFOs starting about two decades ago the internet was more open and free. Now most people go to big social media sites where content can be controlled and removed. The internet now is more settled down and its very easy to get censored or shadow banned if you post anything offensive that is considered 'borderline.' When I first got on the internet I used to troll a lot on music forums and then focused my attention on UFO forums before social media took off. UFO forums is where I noticed I started to receive electronic harassment. A high tone with would fade in and out of my ear followed by sinus pain and TBN (concussion) type symptoms. The year would have been 2003-2004. The reason why I tell an unflattering part of my life is so others can learn from my mistakes in not becoming a target since electronic harassment involves mass surveillance or what is termed warrantless wireless surveillance. My trolling was this sort of behavior that made me a target and I believe most people today are more cautious about what they post to the internet - not only because of the chastising of cancel culture but I believe more people know about mass surveillance and how everything you post can be seen by even prospective employers like having a social media score. This was my impression when applying for jobs - that employers can see if you are on the governments radar, what is termed terrorist watch listing. An easy way to become terrorist watch-listed is by posting to the internet and in my case it was something that may seem trivial to most like UFOs. Then the government can use parallel construction. The police who see you on a watch-list may think you are watch-listed over something else. It's because watch-listing involves a lack of public transparency. The government can just make stuff up about you. This level of phonyness is also apparent on today's internet with bots, sock puppets, shadow banning to decrease viewership and is now something people accept. i.e. The internet is more artificial based on algorithms and click bait. When you're a target there is also a lot of obscene content posted to your social media feed, subject matters that I do not patronize but appear in my feed anyway - implying criminal behavior - this can make you look guilty if you click on the content. I can only speculate social media is a liaison with the intelligence community (IC) or uses intelligence contractors. In researching intelligence contractors (PIAs), which I will get into later, I discovered some are tasked with creating sock puppets. Police have also created fake accounts with help of the FBI called alias identities. When you accept a friend request it could be a cop looking for incriminating evidence or just to monitor a terrorist watch-listed person. The media also looks at a person's social media profile after a news worthy event to look for dirt. Search engines now also play a role in online censorship. Just Google "targeted individuals" and negative dismissive articles by slanted journalist are optimized to appear atop of search results. I posted about my electronic harassment to Youtube and was flamed by sock puppets. A tactic would be to provoke a response where a complaint could be made to remove the video. Then like most targeted individuals (Tis) who looked at analytics they saw their viewership go way down in what they attributed to shadow banning. This is also what I observed, there was less of the use of sock puppets and little to no views as my content became shadow banned. The government of course will excuse online censorship because of what is now called hybrid warfare (Russian troll factories) and irregular warfare (IR) but censorship is a double edged sword - it can also be used to suppress voices. There's computational propaganda where polarized groups can be pitted against each other for political purposes, the Cambridge Analytica scandal was an example. Now during the post-pandemic era people know they were just used as pawns and manipulated by mere statistics where polarization served politicians during a contentious election exploiting (disruptive) dire circumstances. Online censorship and computational propaganda hurt the big social media companies like Facebook, later rebranded Meta, and Twitter rebranded as X because of the culture wars. My targeting began as a response to my research before the internet was about censorship and even before the government publicly embraced UFO alarmism. Now my targeting has turned into non-consensual human experimentation by those into weapons proliferation like directed energy weapons (DEWs) who have taken the on-going abuse for granted, like having no conscience, since there are little consequences. It's a technocratic utilitarian view of society opposing autonomy and free speech that only contributes to government corruption. I stopped posting to social media because of shadow banning, SPAM, and vile user content becoming part of my feed. If you have purchased this book online consider yourself lucky. Some self-published books are not easily seen by popular distributors. I've seen people complain online about this shadow 'book banning' tactic.

Civil War? Or War by Government against Citizens Already Waged.

It's clear our own government has declared a silent war against citizens using mass surveillance. The fear of Libertarians during late-night conspiratorial talk shows was martial law - putting troops in the streets, confiscating guns, and FEMA camps but that is not how its going to happen. It's more like a sniper picking off a citizen one by one. The government and the military establishment can use the information age, militarized law enforcement to find threats and covertly go after you using Fusion Centers, eradicating people (called domestic terrorist) that they don't see fit in a country that's really dictated by them - not the citizen like a type of social Eugenics. Punishing a person with a plausible deniability weapon isn't really respecting the First Amendment; Ninth Amendment and neither is reprisal for peaceably assembling with other TI's holding up a protest sign. Today though, people are increasingly divided (political polarization) and there is less tolerance toward (intolerance) others as more protest based on ideology are marked by violence. Who's to blame? Technocrats - the dehumanizing effects of technology? It's the same people who have waged war on foreign countries, promoted alarmism, and are proponents of violence. These are the same people who use terms like "brave," "hero," when they are really just tyrants. Yes, America can make the same mistake as other countries, where the majority do without and the selfish elite use military might to suppress the population, where there's wide spread rioting, and misery all around. The solution is to scale down war operations overseas and decrease both Federal spending and money to the Department of Defense (DoD) - I know easier said than done but a change in policy, curtailing spending to the Pentagon and Intelligence Community (IC) reforms can be done. It occurs all the time in business. I.e. cutting the fat, downsizing, going back to basics. Neo-liberalism like intelligence contracting can be curtailed, most of which can be done away with entirely to limit abuses that occur out of the public's eye.

The Culprits - The Fear Economy; Alarmism

Who is responsible for me being microwaved? I made a strong case in this book the culprit is the Pentagon. It's the mentality of a war criminal. One could logically conclude that what I have described is no small feat. Most likely not a few stalkers who have been stalking me for a long time using technology but some type of program involving mass surveillance, law enforcement, Neo-liberal intelligence. Followed from state-to-state points to the Federal authorities. I.e Fusion Centers. As much as some in the targeted community try to portray electronic harassment as a 'criminal element,' that is probably not the case, especially in my case. Drug dealers on the streets of New York had a better life than I did and got a good nights sleep. War crimes come from the military; the authorities. Those who can impose their will against a civilian using force. I was targeted and white tortured (no-touch tortured) of a course of two decades. The people doing it appear to follow a schedule/on a payroll. I.e. a government payroll or tax payer funded. Like most they do not have to worry about downsizing. The Federal government and alarmist rhetoric by career politicians has only increased. There's your culprit in plain view. Most are afraid to whistle blow or speak out because of despotism. Targeted in a home or place of dwelling but also the building I was employed in where there was a government related-agency - a very bureaucratic one - the PANYNJ that had some negative spotlight like Bridgegate points to government - Government alarmism over UAP or UFOs. As one targeted individual exclaimed, the expensive involved in 24/7 stalking and surveillance must be enormous like America's trillion dollar national deficit. Then one must ask, if it's no small feat would would be capable for such an undertaking?

Who is actually involved in the monitoring-stalking of citizens and would have access to sophisticated equipment like it is being field tested? The answer to that is the government-defense-intelligence industry looking for rabbits (targets) or guinea pigs to mature directed energy weaponry. I.e directed energy intermediate force capabilities (DE IFC). People's fears of an overbearing government are real and not just conspiracy. As I stated earlier, it's now a big part of the economy. Homeland Security, National Security, Defense-Weapons Industry etc. accounts for a great amount of spending and jobs but also increased the deficient and creates more poor. Then you have to ask why you were targeted, what made you a target, try and determine the cause. Early on it was from posting to UFO forums/ researching UFOs. It became clear someone was monitoring communications. Now we know who: the Pentagon's UFO "Threat Identification Program" (AATIP). It's that threat mitigation thing, now even something trivial as UFO's raises cause for concern because the sky is falling. What's disturbing is the government's wild goose chase, secret lynching of citizens is unethical behavior on so many levels. Human slavery and lynching should have been put behind us. As stated in the introduction. Exploitation, a violation of basic human rights, and government waste - neglecting failing infrastructure which I experienced first hand living in New York City or the increase in the homeless population with unaffordable housing. All because someone wants to pad their wallet using tax dollars playing up threats and acting authoritarian - in fact human exploitation going back to the days of colonialism and slavery is very much driven by economy. Today that is still true. Our American system is built on exploiting people from the days of slavery to domestic terrorism using alarmism and the Homeland Security state.

Below I list of what I consider the most like suspects of my electronic harassment:

Intel Contractors (PIAs); The DoJ & FBI; The Intercept revealed the FBI had become overzealous with what is termed "disruption programs" during the so called War on Terror targeting many types of people it did not want to take to court out of the embarrassment of losing a court case. The FBI has a history of surveillance abuse going back to COINTELPRO and has been accused of entrapment targeting gullible/ hapless losers using informants. The FBI also monitors/ targets people/ groups deemed subversive like its Guardian Threat Tracking System. Palantir also tracks subversives. Leidos helped target foreign terrorist for drone strikes etc.

Law Enforcement: It was revealed the NYPD has non-disclosure agreements with private contractors testing new technology as well as enjoying Federal funds for its counter-terror operations. Lawrence 'Larry' Sanchez, a former CIA officer, was part of a program to surveil the City's Muslim population, later getting into private intelligence going on "rabbit runs." It was also alleged that police departments receive used military grade equipment from the wars in Afghanistan and Iraq. When City Hall in New York proposed a Police Oversight Surveillance Act (POST Act) the NYPD went on the offensive claiming it would inhibit their counter-terror operations with one journalist calling their opposition to more transparency misleading. See-through technology such as body scanners using millimeter waves were tested by the Port Authority and at Penn Station in Manhattan. The police have not been helpful in the plight of TI's as many who go to them for help report involuntary institutionalization. They are part of the Joint Terrorism Task Force (JTTF) and are either directly or indirectly involved. My old job the PANYNJ.gov worked with Fusion Centers and the JTTF and had their own police force (PAPD). There's been a lot of anti-police rhetoric by the woke establishment but I observed that they play a role in the targeting through watch-listing and Fusion Centers.

The CIA: The 2014 Senate Report on CIA Torture has similarities to what targeted individuals describe. Most people think of waterboarding when it comes to Gitmo but threats to family and sleep deprivation are also listed.

Although the CIA is associated with foreign matters, some CIA officials have been involved with law enforcement such as Larry Sanchez who followed and stalked Muslims in New York. I believe torture tactics are used like CIA methods because of the IC's role in private intelligence (PIA) contracting.

Homeland Security (DHS); various counter-terrorism bureaucracies: Many targeted individuals are suspect of Fusion Centers. Information sharing centers that are very secretive and out of the public's eye monitoring the population. The "Watch List" system has been brought up by targeted individuals. Terrorism gives those in authority to test technology and do things that they don't have to be transparent about. Today, the angry Muslim threat that justified the Patriot Act, have all but gone away. Now there is more emphasis on "domestic terrorism" threats.

The Department of Defense (DoD): The beginning of my targeting coincides with Pentagon's UFO Threat Identification Program (AATIP). One of the more public figures associated with that program named Luis Elizondo specialized in counterintelligence. This isn't to imply he was involved but I knew UFO forums were being monitored and someone was alarmed about UFO content - an open source researcher. The Pentagon also kept a list of people, activist deemed a threat in a database named TALON. The DoD proliferates DEWs and has documentation on directed energy intermediate force capabilities (DE IFC).

DARPA: Some targeted individuals will mention DARPA who is connected to the Pentagon or military. Partly due to their developing-scary-new-innovative-weapons image. DARPA are involved in directed energy (DE) technology for military applications. DARPA was involved in the PANYNJ.gov where I was stationed at as a security guard. From what I gather their involvement did have something to do with EMF and critical infrastructure. Radiation were placed around New York City to detect radioactivity. Could they be involved it testing pain-compliance directed energy on civilian targets? They may be involved in what I observed later after moving to Los Angeles and driving way from the city. I could feel directed energy in my car and the effects diminish when driving away from a populated area. Putting more long range directed energy for intermediate force capabilities (IFC) around a city could also point to a defense contractor like Raytheon. I can't entirely rule DARPA out because of their Pentagon connection.

Billionaires: Robert Bigelow, an eccentric billionaire from Las Vegas can be attributed to the Pentagon's UFO Threat Identification Program (AATIP) because of his friendship with then Senator Harry Read. There was tremendous paranoia by Bigelow over foreign adversaries like China and their emerging role in the space and growing interest in UFOs. Billionaires would have the money for stalking like a Harvey Weinstein using Black Cube but more likely persuasion. A person like Bigelow liked relying on the government doing his bidding and I'm sure this could be the case to those are people around him monitoring the internet (UFO Forums) deemed a threat. He himself has a history of paying teams of people, researchers, UFO organizations like MUFON (Star Team) to satisfy his own UFO obsession. There was the rumor that Skinwalker Ranch was actually a testing ground for weapons like directed energy. Other Billionaire's like Peter Thiel, co-founder of PayPal, company Palantir technologies has been cited in articles as keeping track of certain people who are deemed "subversive." Team Themis t destroy the lives of Anonymous hackers. Billionaires like George Soros; Koch Family have been involved in politics. The Rockefeller's had an interest in UFOs (UFO Disclosure Initiative) although appears to be a philanthropist organization.

Defense Contractors: Raytheon and Lockheed Martin expressed interest in further developing non-lethal directed energy like Active Denial. The move toward soldi state directed energy (SS DE). I made the observations when living major cities like LA, Dallas to the country the pain ray dissipates like defense contractors building the weaponry could be putting it around major cities to guard critical infrastructure and use it on TI's. This could be done working in conjunction with law enforcement and or intelligence contractors (PIAs).

Alarming Implications in an Alarmism Era - DE Oppression & Genocide.

The danger of using plausible deniability weaponry out of the public's eye is it can be used for future oppression and not just on a very small isolated segment of the targeted population that is being bullied and marginalized. The general population will find out the ugly truth that they are no match to this cruel oppressive EMF weapon technology that can be used remotely. This could happens if disturbing trends like global warming when there is a tipping point, trouble growing enough crops or there is some sort of global calamity. The general population may realize that they are in a world of haves and have-nots - everyone's needs can not be satisfied. Those who do without will face cruel oppressive technology much like targeted individuals (TI's) are describing with directed energy (DEW) assaults or pain compliance methods. Uprisings will be quelled since guns will no longer be sufficient protection against high tech-weaponry that can quickly immobilize a person. A person's every move will be monitored much like what targeted individuals (TI's) describe since big data, analytics, and info sharing benefit those in positions of power. As one person told me, building big walls on the border can be used to keep people in, instead of stopping immigrants (scapegoats), much like the movie Escape From New York. Others have raised concerns of what will happen when keeping tabs on everyone is not good enough - there's only one way to think and people's thoughts have to be monitored because with a brain chip or detecting brain waves because the wrong type of thinking is subversive (cancel culture). The air you breath and the breaths you take will be taxed and the amount of food you can eat limited as the world gets worse. Will technology be used to exploit humans, suppress reforms, for the all-seeing government's own sinister aim? The military wants to eventually justify using DEWs to kill human targets. What's to stop genocide or ethnic cleansing if a powerful DEW used remotely can vaporize someone with no trace? What if AI took over and everyone was vaporized by DARPA dogs, Terminator robots, and killer drones going door to door? What's the end game of more and more advanced weaponry that the average person (civilian) has no defense against? Not a good one.

Conclusion: I tend to believe the source of my harassment had to do with my internet activity research UFOs and later targeted individuals (TI's). My research was more free-flowing and open source in gathering information. The government believes in lots of secrecy and became alarmed where now government alarmism is a Neo-liberal industry. My research coincided with the Pentagon's own interest in UFO's where UAP was played up as a threat and naturally a person such as myself who was into disclosure/exposing info to the masses became a target. It's also important to note a vocal person part of the Pentagon's program named Luis Elizondo specialized in counterintelligence. This isn't hard evidence of the Pentagon's involvement but a bit too coincidental. Would the Government pick on US citizens regarding UFOs, well as you have read in UFO witness harassment cases the answer is yes. Was I a terrorist? No, but could probably be considered subversive. I tend to be a bit rebellious, if I went about things a different way, maybe a bit more public like becoming a UFO personality then maybe I wouldn't have been targeted. Then again, there's been suspicious deaths of UFO personalities. Of course, this doesn't justify the targeting which is being conducted covertly, considering it was real physical abuse by people using directed energy and probably at a cost to the tax payer, including myself, adding insult to injury like the recent UAP hearings that didn't tell the public a great deal, only that UAP was yet another potential threat to justify government spending. This points out what the targeting is really all about: making money, weapons proliferation. It's been documented that if you allow corporations to create waste and abuse in the name of profit it will happen. i.e. Neo-liberalism (PIAs). It points to the involvement of defense contractors developing DEWs and threat mitigation intelligence contractors (PIAs) and people on a government payroll working out of a Fusion Center (DoJ-law enforcement). I believe that's where the problem lies. There needs to be more transparency in a high-tech world. If anyone is punished then it should be made clear what punishment a citizen will receive, not a free-for-all witch hunt/ weapons ER&D testing because of a watch-listing system that means jobs to knuckle draggers with little to no Liberal Arts education. There also needs to be more accountability on spending. Take money out of the perpetrators hands and they will not be stalking people, maybe they'll reset to UFC fighting or crushing a beer can with their forced instead or other moronic behavior - lis shooting animals for sport. Using directed energy against people like me who are non-violent and do not pose a threat to the population needs to stop or it will be a H.G. Wells Things To Come future not a big-tech utopia.

How to Not be a TI

If you noticed from my testimony my behavior may have made me a target. Here is some advice in how to not become targeted in the age of mass surveillance.

- Try not to look subversive or rebellious online. Big brother is watching. Appear normal, blend in. Post images of cats.

- Pay attention to who the government monitors like activist, conspiracy theorist, hate groups, environmentalist, whistle blowers, loner/losers etc.

- Stay away from certain types of employment that may have ties with the targeting industry. i.e. Government/The Feds, defense, intelligence gathering. Crossing the wrong person there may make you a target or a Government person that does not like you may make you a target.

- If you are a loser limit your participation on social media. People can see if you don't have many friends or well off.

- Don't protest or attend protest. Protest activities are monitored by the authorities.

- Stay away from politics. Everyone feels strongly about their leaders and want to voice their concern or opinion. In reality it's all driven by big money and you voice has little to no impact on things.

Glossary of Terms:

33 Thomas Street: windowless NSA (TITANPOINTE) building that can withstand a nuclear bast.

5 Ds: a military tactic to neutralize a threat. Degrade, Disrupt, Diminish, Discredit…

5150 Code: a code used by cops to involuntarily commit a crazy person for up to 72-hours. A tactic often reported by targeted individuals (Tis) when approaching law enforcement.

9-11: the American emergency phone number to call police. Also ironically, associated with the 2001 terrorist attack.

acquiescence: the reluctant acceptance of something without protest.

Active Denial: an early pain ray maser weapon developed by defense contractor Raytheon for crowd control.

active millimeter wave scanners: direct millimeter wave energy is aimed at a target. A computer interprets the reflected energy to see through clothing.

active shielding: equipment like jammers to disrupt surveillance, EMF, electronic harassment.

active shooter: a term by the DHS to describe mass shooters or what was termed "going postal." Some active shooters claimed to be TI's who snapped. i.e. Aaron Alexis, Myron May FSU shooter.

Advanced Aerospace Threat Identification Program (AATIP): The secret Pentagon study of UFOs during the 2000s but is still allegedly on-going in some facet.

aerial tele-automaton: wireless powered airship concept by Nikola Tesla.

Aerodyne: a wingless aircraft.

affidavit (legal): a sworn or affirmed statement made in writing and signed; if sworn, it is notarized.

agent provocateur: a person from the intelligence community that stirs the pot, creates conflict within a group - usually in foreign operations.

Airship wave: people reported seeing airships in the late 1800s.

Alarmism: a tactic often used by politicians to scare people into accepting policy. I.e the war on terror; mask mandate; UAP threat; WMD's in Iraq; a nuclear weapon in space etc.

aliens: a theoretical advanced life-form from another world depicted in science fiction.

Alien abduction: alleged abduction of people by aliens piloting UFO craft. Became popular in the 1980s with the book Communion and peaked in the 1990s with TV shows like the X-Files.

Alien rejection: some people invited onboard craft for a physical examination were reject and told they were not what the UFO occupants or aliens were looking for.

alien implant: small objects put inside alien abductees by aliens described as a small bee bee or shard of glass. Possibly for tracking like a RFID tag.

algorithms: people are more polarized and manipulated based on their personal preference using data analytics, computational propaganda.

Alt-Right: far right, neoconservative, white nationalist.

American Exceptionalism: a foreign policy believe that the USA is #1, everybody else should be dominated.

anal probe: associated with alien abductions like conducting a colon exam although not frequently reported; the term often used as ridicule.

Anarchism: a political philosophy advocating self-governing societies based on voluntary institutions. Anarchist are often infiltrated by FBI informants.

anomalous: a euphemism word popular with the government as to be be vague and not specific. i.e. anomalous heath Incident, anomalous objects.

ancient astronaut theory: also called ancient aliens, became popular in the 1960s, humans were genetically engineered by aliens in ancient times who left for Planet X.

Anechoic chamber: a room to stop reflections or echoes of either sound or electromagnetic waves.

Angel investor: provides seed money for start up in exchange for some ownership.

Animal rights extremism: believe strongly in the justice for al animals. Often targeted by FBI.

Antifa: super liberal anti-fascist groups that violently clash with the Alt-Right.

anticommunist: the red scare (1919-1920); Cold War (McCarthyism); a resurgence today against Leftist censorship.

antidemocratic conspiracies: the big lie (voter fraud), stop the steal (rigged election), Qanon (deep state).

antigovernment: associated with the hard right movement, anti-federal government, NWO conspiracies.

Anti-vaxxer: a person against COVID vaccines or wearing a mask.

angry Muslim: the antagonist when the so called War on Terror started. They usually scream "Allahu Akbar" and appear fearsome.

alarmist: someone who is considered to be exaggerating a danger and so causing needless worry or panic.

Area 51: A dry lakebed in Nevada administered by Edwards AFB to test stealth craft by Lockheed Martin and also foreign craft. It later became surrounded by UFO lore.

Area 52: allegedly Nevada's other base at Tonopah Test Range (TTR) or Dugway Proving Ground in Utah.

asylum seeker: seeks refuge to a foreign country because of political persecution and serious human rights violations.

Automatic writing: some unknown force writes words or drawings using a person's hands.

autonomous DEW battles: A robot battle using DE measured on millisecond timescales, which by some estimates is faster than a human can think.

avatar account: a fake online ID or persona used for stalking a target by a private intelligence contractor.

Attorney General: heads the DoJ.

Baker Act: A Florida law - the same as involuntary institutionalization or 5150.

Beam-powered propulsion: also known as directed energy (DE) propulsion, is a class of aircraft or spacecraft propulsion that uses energy beamed to the spacecraft. e.g. laser propelled Lightcraft.

Benefits corporation: is a type of for-profit corporate entity to make a positive impact on society.

Behavior Analysis Unit (BAU): a department at the FBI that studies behavior of criminals, killers etc.

behavioral modification: the theory that some targeted individuals are being tortured as a means of control; changing their behavior.

Big Pharma: conspiracy theory that believes the pharmaceutical industry operates for greedy sinister purposes.

back door access: covert method of bypassing normal authentication and encryption methods to gain access to a computer.

bioeffects: effects of radio waves and high-powered microwaves on the human body.

bioethics: ethics of biological research whether it be medicine, weaponry, etc.

Bioethics Commission: A defunct advisory board that briefed the president on bioethical issues.

Biological warfare: also known as chemical warfare. There has been a resurgence like used in the Syrian civil war (2012) and conspiracies around the Wuhan lab leak.

black bag: unauthorized search or break in to someones house to go through their belongings.

black hat: internet hacker the malicious intent. White hats or hackers who believe they are doing good.

blepharospasm: eyelid spasms due to external stimuli like chemical irritants or directed energy.

Bootstrapping: a business from scratch without investment and minimal capital.

Borderline Personality Disorder (BPD): a person that is emotionally unstable, associated with criminals.

Buoyant aircraft: an aerostat, airship, balloon, semi-buoyant aircraft. I.e. a craft that uses buoyancy.

branch-off civilization: advanced civilizations of the past or those part of secret technology created a more advanced civilization off-planet explaining UFOs.

brain-computer interface: control something like a computer mouse through thoughts by a microchip implant to brain. e.g. Neuralink

Brain Invaders: a conspiracy cable TV program episode from 2009 by Jesse Ventura that looked at targeted individuals. I.e. microwave harassment, V2K etc.

brainwashing: the human mind can be altered or controlled by certain psychological techniques.

CACI International: Fedral contractor alleged to have been invloved with the Abu Grahib prisoner abuse scandal as well as the known or suspected terrorist watchlisting system.

cancel culture: a Leftist political, angry mob mentality, peer pressure tactic to chastise those in society who say something offensive or have a racist emotional outburst.

cattle mutilation: a type of animal mutilation involving cattle where ranchers reported mutilations that appeared unusual like the blood drained, laser precision cuts, lack of decomposition. Associated with UFOs.

corona discharge: creates hum and blue glow around high voltage lines.

cell towers: there has been an increase in cell towers that have 5G and emit RF, microwave emissions sometimes disguised as a tree

censorship: the ability to stop free and open expression from reaching the public. Today often referred to as online censorship.

charlatan: a person falsely claiming to have impressive credentials or background.

chemical irritant: a type of chemical or substance is used to irritate the body. I.e. Itching powder, pepper spray, poison ivy.

chemtrails: the conspiracy believe that toxic agents like metal particles are spread in the air by large aircraft leaving trails in the sky for weather mitigation.

CIA: Intelligence agency that deals with mostly foreign matters. Called the Agency; The Company. Involved in Spy planes, covert-actions, Gitmo torture.

Citizen App. A popular smartphone app that monitors police scanners and members film crime scenes.

Cilunar orbit: unwatched area between the moon and earth.

Class action: people will group together in a law suit to sue a corporation.

clairvoyance: the UFO occupants had supposed faculty of perceiving things or beyond normal sensory ability. A popular term during the Contactee era.

code names: military names for programs like project second story; project snowbird; project moon dust; project horse fly.

COINTELPRO: counter-intelligence by the FBI against suspected communist, and the civil rights movement during the Cold War.

community policing: some targeted individuals believe that community policing or neighborhood watch groups are complicit in their targeting, infraGuard etc.

conductive energy device (CED): a device that conducts electricity when it hits he skin like a taser used by law enforcement.

confidence trickster: like scam artist, defraud and deceive people believing something that is not true to take advantage of them.

confirmation bias: see things in a way to favors your own beliefs or prejudices instead of being objective.

conspiracy theorist: the belief that there's something sinister, afoot involving the powers that be - made popular on the internet (Alex Jones) and late night talk radio.

conspiracy to commit: charges to conspire charges are often used against people by the authorities. I.e. conspiracy to commit a crime.

Contactees: writers like George Admaski from the 1950s-1960s who claimed to have contact with human looking flying saucer occupants that processed clairvoyance who came from planets in our own solar system.

counter-intelligence: to neutralize or disrupt activities that threaten national interest like using disinformation, discrediting efforts, a covert action.

Counter-terrorism: efforts by the government to stop terrorist activity.

covert-action: a secretive action to neutralize a citizen deemed a threat, usually death.

Cover-up: the belief that the government is hiding something like evidence of crashed saucers, alien bodies. E.g. Roswell

cracker: a cyber-security term to describe a computer hacker, someone who gets access to passwords.

Crimes Against Humanity: are Torture, Enslavement; Extermination; Murder et al.

criminal element: the element of our economy involved in illegal activity or criminal enterprise.

critical infrastructure: described by the DHS as a major city's power grid, water et al.

critical thinking: the objective analysis and evaluation of an issue in order to form a judgment using, the study of inductive and deductive reasoning.

crop circles: mysterious pattern imprints done to crop fields that some claim are hoaxes and some believe by UFOs.

cruel and unusual punishment = punishment that is considered unacceptable due to the suffering, pain, or humiliation it inflicts on the person subjected to the sanction.

cyber-bullying: When a person bullies another person online. Some teens have committed suicide of cyber bullying.

cyber-stalking: A person who becomes obsessed with someone online like a social media influencer, public figure, or former lover and stalks them on the internet.

cyber-torture: a pseudo-term proposed to the UN to highlight the threat of technologies in the cyber age that can be used as torture.

dark web: encrypted internet associated with illegal activity like pushing drugs, sex crimes.

death threats: threats of violence toward a politician, the President, or police officer can cause a person to become arrested or investigated by the secret service.

deep state: a conspiratorial term describing a clandestine network of members of the federal government and intel community against Donald Trump.

denial: the act not wanting to acknowledge something disturbing is real.

de-humanize: to take away qualities that makes us human like compassion toward others observed in techno-centric societies.

delusional: a false belief associated with mental disorders.

delusions of grandeur: the belief that a person is more important than they really are and embraced by some conspiracy theorist.

despotism: the exercise of absolute power, especially in a cruel and oppressive way.

Detox: some TI's believe a detox bath is necessary to preserve their health and mitigate some of the effects of their harassment.

DHS SAFETY Act: legal liability protections for antiterrorism technologies designed by Homeland Security contractors.

direct action: strikes, demonstrations, or other forms to protest.

Directed Energy (DE): used to describe weapon technology like lasers, masers, RF, microwave.

Directed Energy Weapons (DEWs): associated with high-energy lasers (HEL); high-powered microwaves (HPM). Active Denial using millimeter waves (mmWave) is less-than lethal.

directional sound: sound that can narrowly focused at a person. E.g. directional sound device.

dirigible: a rigid structure airship popular in the early 20th century. I.e. Hindenburg, Zeppelin.

disclosure (movement): activism by UFO conspiracy theorist that the government should spill the beans on aliens, UFOs, a cover-up.

disinformation: mix fallacy with some semblance of truth to mislead.

disposition matrix: used to describe black sites, kill list, predator drone strike programs.

disruption programs: the FBI tries to disrupt a person or suspected terrorist activities without taking them to court out of fear of losing a court case.

domestic terrorist: citizens accused or suspected of terrorism by the government, usually not the angry Muslim like 9-11 but homegrown threats.

dot com bubble: a period of economic growth during the late 90s because of internet web sites/innovation.

doxxing: posting someones personal info online with malicious intent

dragnet: a sting operation where a front organization or fake adds attract people later to charged with a crime. Usually in prostitution.

drone: a small aircraft that is remote controlled and has cameras or weapons if its military grade.

EBE: A term referring to an alien. i.e. extraterrestrial biological entity, from the MJ-12 UFO conspiracy theory.

elder abuse: abuse of the elderly or senior citizens.

election fraud: the ability to sway elections by unscrupulous means. I.e. cooking the books; mail in votes from illegitimate voters, ballot harvesting.

electromagnetic warfare (EW): warfare using weapons in the EMF spectrum. I.e. directed energy (DE).

Electromagnetic interference (EMI): electrical equipment that interferes with other electronic equipment like your TV or radio.

electronic harassment: a figurative term by targeted individuals (Tis) to described directed energy or electromagnetic weapon assaults, V2K etc.

electronic tagging: the attaching of electronic markers to people or goods for monitoring purposes, e.g., to track offenders under house arrest or to deter shoplifters, ankle monitor, RFID chip.

electronic warfare (EW): associated with the military. i.e. jamming devices.

Electromagnetic hypersensitivity (EHS): sensitivity to electromagnetic fields; electrical equipment.

ELF: Low frequency radio waves usually for communication of submarines. Aaron Alexis had extremely low frequency (My ELF weapon) etched on his gun but also according to articles spoke of microwave harassment.

emerging technologies: newer R&D technologies often unregulated. I.e. robots, IE, DEWs, nanotechnologies et al.

EMF measurements: are measurements of ambient (surrounding) electromagnetic fields that are performed using particular sensors or probes, such as EMF meters.

EMP: electromagnetic pulse weapons can damage electronics.

emotional distress: under "intentional infliction" law, is distress so substantial or long-lasting that no reasonable person should be expected to bear it.

emotional intelligence: relate to others in a positive away with the feelings in mind.

emotionally disturbed: a term often used by law enforcement to describe a person's erratic behavior; usually someone very upset and or on drugs.

empirical evidence: using observation to support evidence.

Engineering Research and Development (ER&D): new things are created, tested, and applied toward the subject to gauge the effectiveness.

entrapment: setting people up for terrorism plots by the FBI.

ESP: reception of information not gained through physical senses.

Extraterrestrial Hypothesis (ETH): UFOs are piloted by interstellar aliens like depicted in science fiction.

eugenics: creating a race with favorable characteristics such as intelligence, skin color, appearance. e.g the Nazi master-race.

euphemism: a tactic by the government to downplay torture or directed energy using more vague words. I.e extraordinary rendition; anomalous health effect.

expat: a US citizens that leaves the country living abroad.

Extrajudicial: bypassing due process to prosecute someone. I.e Death squads, lynchings, terrorist watch list, kill list, mercenaries.

FBI: intelligence agency involved in domestic criminal/terrorism maters; Federal law enforcement.

false arrest: when police arrest a person and fabricate evidence usually to cover-up wrong doing.

fake accounts: law enforcement, police, contractors will create fake online personas to monitor people. I.e. Avatar operators, alias identities, sock puppets.

fake news: a pejorative term used by Trump implying the mainstream media is bias, politically motivated, even fabricating false stories like a form of character assassination.

fantasy prone: a debunker explanation to explain alien abduction as people who believe in their own fantasies.

Faraday Cage: a metallic material coper that is grounded and is used for a surrounding or canopy to exclude electrostatic and electromagnetic influences or block EMF.

Federal Air Marshal: also sky marshal, protects passengers and crew from security threats aboard aircraft.

Federal Sunshine Laws: regulations requiring public disclosure of government agency meeting and records.

fight or flight response: the instinctive physiological response to a threatening situation, which readies one either to resist forcibly or to run away.

First Amendment: right to free speech, free press, peaceably to assemble.

First Amendment audit: people with cameras on public property who provoke confrontations with angry law enforcement then file lawsuits.

FISA Amendment Act: foreign intelligence surveillance act that is often cited by targeted individuals. Similar to the Patriot Act enacted after 9-11 giving the government a 'gloves off' approach waving peoples rights.

Five observables: STARCOMS (Space Force) five techno-signatures of UAP (UFOs). i.e. gravity defying behavior; low observability on radar and other sensors 3) sudden accelerations 4) hypersonic without sonic booms 5) trans-medium travel between air-sea-space.

FOIA (Freedom Of Information Act): Watch-dog groups and journalist use the FOIA to try retrieve documents that divulge info not known by the public.

foreign body sensation: the sensation of a speck of dirt on your eye though nothing can be found to cause it.

flag waver: someone overly patriotic into nationalism, troop worshipping and will go along with any war - the flag is always on display.

Flying saucer: a term that became popular after the Kenneth Arnold sighting describing a circular-wing or lenticular-shaped craft. Depicted in science fiction.

flying wing aircraft: a stealthy aircraft missing a tail or
fuselage that looks like angled wings chevron,
boomerang.

folklore, legend, fairy tales: old world fictitious stories
with fictitious creature like fairies, elf's, dragons, giants.

forced speech: some TI's believe they are forced to say
certain words that can be degrading.

front organization: an organization like a non-profit that
really serves the intelligence community.

Fusion Center: information sharing centers to keep track
of citizens by the DHS that are in locations across the US
kept secret from the public.

gang stalking: a term by targeted individuals to describe
coordinated groups of people, perhaps surveillance role
players, or intel contractors who overtly follow and stalk
a person as a form of intimidation/ pressure tactic.

gas attack: Some TI's believe a gas irritant is used to make the feel sick with severe sinus migraines etc.

gaslighting: a psychological manipulative tactic by others to you question your own sanity.

generational abduction: alien abductees who believe alien abductions span generations following a genetic line.

Gauss Meter: displays electromagnetic wave measurements in Gauss (G), milliGauss (mG), milliTesla (mT) or microTesla (µT) units.

genetic engineering: theoretical concept of using DNA to engineer favorable traits in a species.

ghost: a term for special FBI special agents who follow someone on foot or traffic without being detected.

ghost fliers: mysterious aircraft seen in England, Eastern Europe like Finland during the 1930s.

ghosting: ending communication with a person with no
explanation by prospective employers, friends.

Gitmo: Guantanamo Bay detention camp.

Government bullying: occurs when the government feels
threatened where a citizen may be treated harsher than
other citizens.

Government Dysfunction: politicians put their agenda
ahead of public interest and the well being of the country

Grays: short gray skinned aliens associated with alien
abductions. Became popular in the 1980s and 1990s.

The Guardian Threat Tracking System: FBI reporting
system that tracks threats. It took over the DoD's TALON
in 2007.

gullible: a person willing too willing to believe in tall-tales; conspiracies.

hacktivist: hacker activist like Barrett Brown who exposed private intel contractors and was targeted by the FBI.

hallucination: seeing something that's not there usually by taking LSD, mushrooms, or by mental illness.

Hanger 18: part of UFO lore where UFO crash debris was stored at Wright Field AFB by crash retrieval crews.

hang up calls: calls meant to pester, intimidate, with no real caller on the other end of the line.

handler: the leader of the perpetrators giving orders.

hate crime: violence toward a person because of ethnic or racial prejudice.

hate groups or domestic hate groups: groups or organizations that show prejudice, hate other types of people. Targeted by SPLC, The FBI.

hoaxes: there are many hoaxed UFO sightings and reports or CGI fakes online.

hoaxers: a person who hoaxes something like a UFO to get attention or online viewership.

hologram: the projection of a 3D image usually translucent in appearance.

honey trap: an attractive woman who is really agent uses sex appeal to set up a person.

horizontal organization: prominent with anarchism, no real leader instead teamwork, collaboration, bartering.

hostile working environment: changes in the colleagues behavior usually toxic in the workplace or also called workplace mobbing.

huckster: hawker, peddler using opportunism. e.g. I investigated UAP for the Pentagon or MoD now have a private UAP venture, make TV appearances, somewhat of a UFO celebrity.

human rights: rights inherent to all human beings like life, liberty, freedom from slavery and torture, free speech, right to work and education.

human trafficking: trade of humans for exploitative/nefarious purposes.

HUMINT: military terminology for gathering human intelligence like infiltrating a group; using an informant.

Hybrids: the result of sexual alien abductions where there are offspring.

hybrid warfare: unconventional warfare not involving a traditional army to fight against like hacking, manipulating social media.

hybrid airship: powered airship that obtains some of its life from lighter-than-air (LTA). Dynostat is a fixed wing hybrid airship and rotastat is rotary wings.

Idiot savant: a person gifted in one area like math but lacking in other areas like social skills.

IFO: a vast majority of UFO sightings can be explained by natural, mundane phenomenon. i.e stars, satellites, a sun dog, ball lightning, Chinese lantern, drone, conventional aircraft.

Incubus: a demon in folklore that seeks sexual intercourse with sleeping women.

Industrial espionage: trade secrets leaked to a competitor of foreign government like China.

infraGuard: private industry partnerships with the FBI to report anything suspicious.

informant: snitches for the FBI that try to incriminate someone; they appear like civilians and try to befriend others, noted for infiltrating groups.

insider threat: someone within a company that divulges unauthorized company secrets or a whistle blower.

Inspector general: receiving and investigating complaints of corruption, conflicts of interest etc.

Institutional abuse: can occur in cults, religious institutions, prisons mental wards, nursing homes.

Intelligence Community (IC): usually referred the alphabet agencies. I.e. NSA, FBI, CIA, DIA, DHS et al.

Intermediate force capabilities: the use if non-lethal weapon force to achieve a desired result.

interrogatories (legal): written questions propounded by one party and served on an adversary, who must provide written answers thereto under oath.

interstellar object: comets, asteroids not from are solar system that passes through the inner solar system.

involuntary institutionalization: also involuntary commitment, when a person is deemed crazy by the police and held for psychological examination against their will. Also 5150 or Baker Act.

ionizing radiation: stuff that people call radiative, harmful.

Ionocraft: small model craft made by hobbyist that are propelled by ion wind.

Irritant gases: gases from chemicals that irritate the lungs, breathing.

Itching powder: often used as a prank but could be used to irritate someone.

Job screeners: TI's report employment difficulty like
having a negative social media score from job screening
services connected to the spook contracting world that
can see more than a criminal record. E.g. ClearForce.

Joint Terrorism Task Force (JTTF): a fusion center
collaboration by the FBI and law enforcement to
investigate and thwart suspected terrorist.

knuckle dragger: a military or special forces person who
is not an intellectual, well cultured.

KST File: Known Suspected Terrorist file that law
enforcement, the TSA/Feds have access to by accessing a
watch-list database.

KURBARK Manual: A 1963 CIA counterintelligence
interrogation manual details torture techniques like shock,
isolation, threats, sensory deprivation.

laser-plasma technology: a theoretical way to confuse
radar and fighter jets using laser plasma to create a
hologram.

law enforcement: armed uniform people on a government payroll that enforce the laws.

Less-Lethal Weapon: An updated, nicer term for non-lethal weapon.

Libertarians: A political philosophy that believes in principles like political freedom, autonomy, individualism.

LIDAR: uses lasers and radar for measuring distance.

lone wolf: also called a lone-offender by the FBI is a person, usually a loner, acting alone in some plot.

lore: traditional belief of mythical figure past down from generation. e.g. the easter bunny; tooth fairy.

loser: an unambitious person who fails respectable achievement by society standards; is usually insecure around others.

MKULTRA: a mind experiment program against unknowing citizens during the cold war using involving LSD.

machine learning (ML): focuses on the using data and algorithms to enable AI to imitate the way that humans learn, gradually improving its accuracy.

magic: something that looks impossible but there's a trick to it or slight-of-hand. i.e. levitation, diapering act, card game trick.

magnetometer: is a device that measures magnetism—the direction, strength, or relative change of a magnetic field at a particular location.

magnetron: an electron tube for amplifying or generating microwaves, used in microwave ovens.

Manchurian Candidate: A person can be psychologically manipulated in carrying out an assassination. A concept popular during the Cold War.

Mandela Effect: a false memory where different people remember the same thing.

Marian apparition: manifestations of the Virgin Mary.

marginalization: to make a victim or person seem less important, not credible.

martyr: a person willing to die for their cause.

maser: microwave laser that is invisible to the naked eye.

Maslow's Hierarchy of Needs: in psychology basic need for well-being like safety, love and belonging, esteem and self- actualization.

maverick: an unorthodox independent person like an inventor.

mental health: an explanation often cited by the media to explain disturbing actions by an individual because of their mental condition.

microwave harassment: reported by targeted individuals where RF weaponry is suspected in their targeting causing pain and sleep deprivation.

microwave hearing: also termed the Frey effect or V2K.

microwave pulses: pulsed microwave attacks was speculated in the Havana Syndrome.

militias: militarized civilians usually part of asymmetrical warfare.

The Milgram Experiment: a psychological experiment to see if a person would apply electric shock to another when instructed to by an authority figure.

millimeter waves: radio waves in the millimeter band. Used in Raytheon's pain ray weapon and body scanners like at the Airport.

millimeter wave scanners: used for body imaging such as airport screeners. They come in two varieties, active and passive.

militarization: when police take on the appearance and practices of the military like its counterterrorism operations.

mind control: there have been experiments in mind control like MKULTRA during the Cold War and reported in alien abductions.

misinformation: false information to deceive or out of ignorance.

Morgellons disease: a condition leaving lesions or strings coming out of the skin caused by toxins or autoimmune disease. Disputed in the medical world

Myokymia: rapid involuntary twitching of the eyelid.

Nano particles: some TI's believe in the conspiracy that nano materials are put inside their body and part of their electronic harassment or explains Morgellons disease. Although it seems unlikely there is the study of nano medicine.

National Institute of Justice (NIJ.gov): The ER&D arm of the Justice Department who was involved in the development of the Assault Intervention Device (AID).

national security: information that the government deems important to the security of the country. Secret documents, confidential information.

National security letter (NSL): an old tactic by the FBI to get a warrant to monitor a person through they ISP, banks, employer etc.

Neo-Liberalism: privatizing industry that was once government like national security, social services etc.

nervous breakdown: also called mental breakdown is
when a person locks up unable to function normally
usually feeling overwhelmed.

NFC (Near Frequency Communication) devices: chips
that can be implanted into a pet or animal and detected at
point-blank range with a scanner that uses an
electromagnetic frequency to power up the implanted
microchips.

noise campaigns: some targeted individuals believe loud
vehicles intentionally pass by them to disturb the peace
part of on-going noise harassment campaigns. Loud
torture music has been used by the CIA at Gitmo, a
hitting jail bars with a metal object to disturb sleep used
in prisons.

no-fly list: a category of the watch-list where a person
deemed dangerous can't fly.

no-touch torture: a term by the CIA to inflict pain without
physical restraint/touching; described in the KUBARK
manual during the Cold War.

non-consensual experimentation: targeted individuals (Tis) believe that they are not only being harassed but experimented on as their reaction to (ER&D) new things is being tested.

non-disclose agreement: a signed agreement between parties to not divulge information.

non-investigative subject: on a terrorist watch-list but not to the extreme as no-fly list.

non-ionizing radiation: EMF that is not radioactive like microwaves, wireless internet.

Non-Lethal Weapons: weapons also termed less-than lethal designed to inflict pain that don't cause physical injury. Mace spray, taser, rubber bullets, bean bags rounds, baton, LRAD, Active Denial etc.

notice of claim (legal): a paper required in the lawsuit process to be sent to the city or public authority when a person claims a city caused the person damage.

ocular irritation: dry eyes, burning of the eyes.

off-the shelf (COTS) components: RF systems can be made with off-the-shelf components through electronic suppliers. Magnetron, Waveshaper etc

Obols: orange balls of light or metallic spheres associated with UFO probes.

Oort cloud: outer edge of solar system that has ice.

open-source information (OSINT): Intelligence term for gathering data using open sources.

opiod crisis: tens of thousands of deaths resulting from prescription opiod abuse across the US. Blamed on the pharmaceuticals; pain prescription pills; the drug trade.

oppression: prolonged cruel or unjust treatment or control.

pacifist: a person who does not like war or violence against others. I.e. conscientious objector.

Palantir Technologies: A CIA funded Sensitive Compartmented Information (SCI) and block chain encrypted private intelligence company that's into predictive policing using data mining/ shared databases.

panic attack: A sudden episode of intense uncontrolled fear and anxiety.

paroxysmal coughing: coughing fits like the whooping cough caused by an external source or underlying health conditions.

The Parallax View: a movie involving conspiracies and assassination.

Parallel construction: a law enforcement tactic of illegally attaining evidence like snooping and building a separate case against the suspect that's admissible in court.

Parrilla (torture): electrical torture using a conductive energy device like electrocution or tasers.

Particle beam (PB) weapons: electron or charged & neutral particle beams have deeper penetration in materials, such as through metals that shield electronics but are limited to close range or high-altitude operations, and secondary ionizing radiation.

passive millimeter wave scanners: create images using only ambient radiation and radiation emitted from the human body and objects.

passive shielding: material used to shield or absorb directed energy. I.e. RF absorbers used in an anechoic chamber

Patriot Act: emergency legislation to strip a citizens rights away including privacy because of the War on Terror following 9-11-01.

peeping Tom laws: laws against citizens looking into a neighbors house even if the person looking is suspicious of them.

permabans: permanent ban, a term used during the dot com era because of moderation on E-Mail mailing list and internet message boards.

perp: a term used by targeted individuals for perpetrators - people who stalk; harass.

persona: a term used by private intel contractors for a person playing role or character, surveillance role players.

plaintiff (legal): a person who brings a case against another in a court of law.

plausible deniability: an action that can be denied because there is little to no physical evidence. Used by governments, the military, politicians.

police brutality: when police become physical and use too much force or a police beating.

political corruption: is the use of powers by government officials or their network contacts for illegitimate private gain. E.g LA city hall, the corrupt sheriff.

Private Intelligence Agency (PIA): contractors who do the spy work of intelligence agencies using connections in Washington to win contracts.

Private Military Company (PMC): modern-day mercenaries or armed contractors filling the military's role in hostile/combat situations.

Private Security Company: termed a PPO is California, an employer of security guard's to deter theft, ward off intruders, access control, personal protection.

project blue beam: a conspiracy belief in a planned false flag alien invasion using holographic technology to dupe the public.

Project Sheriff: a short-ranged (Active Denial) non-lethal millimeter wave weapon for urban warfare placed on the back of a Stryker vehicle that was tested in in 2005.

Pseudo-science: claims that appear scientific but don't meet the scientific method.

psychological break: when a person snaps, becomes violent.

psychological warfare: head games to keep a person feeling down, oppressed.

Psychotropic weapons: a weapon designed to remotely interfere and manipulate a person's mind. E.g. subliminal advertisement creating a Manchurian Candidate.

PTSD: acronym for post-traumatic stress disorder, usually a condition suffered by military vets.

Pulp magazine: an early science fiction magazine like Amazing Stories from 1919 by Hugo Gernsback.

Quantico, Virginia: campus where FBI personal trains including the FBI laboratory, operational technology division et al.

quiet hiring/firing/quitting: given little work hours after hired hoping employee will quit, not given any hours or, lack of job fulfillment b employee without officially quitting.

rabbit: the person being targeted. The term comes from a paper rabbit used in target practice.

rabbit run: also termed running the rabbit in the military. Groups of people chase a target (rabbit) on the move.

radiation dermatitis: a skin condition, usually side effect of radiotherapy cancer treatment.

radiation otitis media (OM): or Otitis media are side effects of radiotherapy of the head and neck regions causing tinnitus.

RAND Corporation: military think tank into topics like DEWs.

redacted document: a sensitive document from FOIA that has black lines through information government doesn't want to disclose.

remote viewing: a pseudoscience belief in sensing an object remotely.

Resonator: a component to a sonic weapon (USW) that emits an ultrasonic vibration field.

RF: is radio frequency, also microwave like RF towers.

RF Weapons: another name for directed energy weapons (DEWs) using microwave.

remedy (legal): is a form of court enforcement of a legal right resulting from a successful civil lawsuit.

remote neural monitoring: a conspiracy belief by some targeted individuals that their thoughts are being monitored.

Reptilians: also called lizard people, humanoid reptiles depicted in science function and conspiracies.

Sandia National Laboratories: tested a smaller version of Active Denial using the using the repel effect and goodbye effect in 2006.

sanction: in the social sciences, is similar to be punished to enforce behavioral standards. E.g. Charges against January 6 rioters on the Capital.

satellite harassment: some TI's believe in the conspiracy theory that they are receiving directed energy assaults by iridium satellites controlled by the Space Force out of Vandenberg AFB or HAARP technology.

satellite weapons: some believe some satellites are weaponized.

scapegoat: someone to blame especially if things are not going well. i.e. police, domestic terrorist, politician, foreign power.

scaler waves: some TI's use the pseudo term scaler waves as an alternative to conventional directed energy. This may be true with sonic weapons because sound is used.

schizophrenia: a mental health condition often characterized by a person having hallucinations; hearing voices.

science fiction: entertainment that fictionalizes technology, unproven science. I.e. wormholes, time travel, aliens, spaceships. Early sincere fiction was by Jules Verne; H.G. Wells.

Scientism: people who pay strict coherence to the scientific method like those in Academia or scientist.

secrecy classifications: used to keep information like documents on a need-to-know basis. I.e. classified, secret, top secret.

secret societies: secretive gatherings by the powerful participating in rituals.

Secret weapons hypothesis (SWH): UFOs are really experimental, secret aircraft.

security clearance: a clearance to access sensitive national security information by government, military, private-affiliated contractors.

see-through technology: devices that can see through clothing, walls to detect objects.

Senate Select Committee on Intelligence (SSCI) on CIA torture: A report from 2012 that detailed the CIA's detention and interrogation program and its use of various forms of torture.

sexual-touching: when a targeted individual believes they
are being violated sexually by their harassers using
DEWs. i.e. penetration of private areas; forced
ejaculation.

Sheriff Buford Pusser: a legendary one man army against
illegal activity and corruption.

shill: a person who pretends to give an impartial
endorsement of something in which they themselves have
an interest or fake advocate by the government.

The Shock Doctrine: a theory by liberal author Naomi
Klein that argues there is a strategy to exploit a national
crises to push through controversial policies like going to
war in Iraq following 9-11, the Patriot Act, etc.

shadow ban: when social media giants allegedly mask or
hide a person's post from regular feeds due to offensive
content deemed borderline so they get little to no views.

Silent Guardian: smaller version of Raytheon's Active Denial System (ADS) that was going to be truck mounted.

silent weapon: another name for directed energy.

Skin-irritant: material that irritates the skin; causes itching, rashes. I.e. itching powder, poison ivy.

SKYNET: a program by the NSA that performs machine learning analysis on communications data to extract information about possible terror suspects.

smart meters: a modern day meter reader attached to a house. People paranoid over EMF exposure or have electromagnetic hypersensitivity (EHS) claim smart meters emit harmful RF frequencies.

skeletons-in-the-closet: a secret taboo part of a person's life that isn't disclosed to others around them. i.e. Belief in conspiracies, the occult, sexual fetish.

sleep deprivation: a common torture tactic to lesson a person's quality and mental health like a targeted person always feeling tired, fatigued by having their sleep disturbed.

Special Surveillance Group: also referred to Ghost "G's" by the FBI who follow a suspect by car or foot without the suspects knowing.

Special Access Programs (SAPs): also USAPs (unacknowledged), need-to know deep dark secret programs.

Social Media Exploitation (SOMEX): fake online ID's created by FBI to look for suspects and share with Fusion Centers.

Sonic Weapons: also termed USW (ultrasonic weapons) a non-lethal weapon using sound. i.e. the LRAD. Initially speculated in the Havana Syndrome.

sousveillance: when a person being monitored, stalked records the stalker using a camera, recording device, etc.

Southern Poverty Law Center (SPLC): a quasi-government non-profit organization that keeps track of so called hate groups. The name derives from a negative Southern stereotype.

sovereign citizen: a pseudo belief that a person releases themselves from government laws and taxes. Associated with scams.

Sovereign immunity: a general rule that you can not sue the government unless it's a tort like a negligent government employee causing injury.

social justice warrior (SJW): angry left-wing activist who believe in social justice causes and have highly political correct views. The antithesis of the far-right.

social engineering: associated with phishing scams, tricking people to compromise personal data through E-mail, online persuasion.

socialist: associated with the far-left in politics, Karl Marx.

solid-state: electronics that uses semiconductor devices making for compactness and portability.

Solid-state Active Denial Technology (SS-ADT): Also called the skid-plate system was a newer version of Active Denial that is solid state.

solid-state directed energy (SS DE): directed energy has evolved to become solid state making it less cumbersome.

solid-state lasers: semiconductor based lasers that are no longer the big gas or chemical lasers from the past.

spear phishing: text messaging or phone calls that trick target into clicking on malicious link. e.g. Pegasus spyware.

Space Force: a new branch of the military focusing on space like satellite weapon threats, space weapons, space anomalous objects (UFOs), military space capabilities,

Space UFOs: unidentified objects seen on NASA footage or UFO craft allegedly seen in space by astronauts, whistle blowers. E.g. Gary McKinnon

Space UFO Euphemisms: new euphemisms were created by the government (Space Force) to describe UFOs detected in space like 'abnormal observables,' 'patterns of life,' 'orbital unknowns,' 'anomalous objects.'

specimen: samples for laboratory analysis. UFO occupants could be seen gathering soil samples, earth specimen

spectrum analyzer: gives a visual measurement of the magnitude of an input signal versus frequency within the full frequency range of the instrument.

stake-out box: groups of cars driven by FBI agents try to box a person is who is being followed.

stalking: watching or following someone without their knowing.

stateless: a US citizen that renounces their citizenship and has no where to go lacking protection by the government.

statute of limitations: a time frame when a lawsuit can be filed.

sternutatory: a sneeze inducing agent like sneezing powder.

StingRay: older snooping technology that tricks a phone to think it's communicating with a cell tower like wiretapping.

subversive: seeking or intended to subvert an established system or institution.

suicide by cop: people who approach cops and pull out a weapon in order to be shot.

summons (legal): a plaintiff's written notice, in a specific form, delivered to the parties being sued, that they must answer the plaintiff's attached complaint within a specific time.

Sun dog: atmospheric bright spot optical illusion because of the sun.

supernatural: some believe UFOs cross into the realm of the supernatural or metaphysical, even physical manifestations of the imagination world while others see this as pseudoscience. I.e. author Jacques Vallee.

surveillance role players (SRVs): people who role play in training situations involving surveillance operations, hired by intel contractors.

survey meter: hand-held ionizing radiation measurement instruments like a Geiger counter.

Suspicious Activity Report (SAR): reports reporting citizens to Fusion Centers. I.e. eGuardian System

sweep: is a bust by the FBI or law enforcement to reel in unsuspecting targets.

tag: similar to an implant or tracking device, like tagging an animal in the wild to tracks it's location. E.g. air tag.

tagging, tracking, locating (TTL): also termed HTTL is placing a tracker on a target suspect or terrorist, their equipment or vehicles and spying on them using satellite imagery and other sensors. Used by intelligence contractor Blackbird Technologies, now Raytheon Blackbird, also by SOCOM with special forces soldiers.

TALON (Threat and Local Observation Notice) reports: a database including lists of anti-war groups and people who have attended anti-war rallies, peace activist by the DoD from 2002-2007

Terahertz (THz): also called sub millimeter between infrared and microwave is used in cameras that see-though clothing, walls,

targeted individual (TI): people who believe they are the targets of covert harassment.

targeted family: an intimidation tactic used to punish or silence a target.

taser (conducted-energy device): a non lethal weapon used by cops to subdue an unruly person using a jolt of electricity.

taser abuse: when police get carried away using taser's on a person out of anger.

technocrat: people who advocate, worship technology. Techno-innovation is the answer to all our problems.

telepathy: ability to communicate through the mind and not using words.

terrorism: associated with violent acts by radicalized people who oppose the government. Some say the term is political.

terrorist watch-listed - terrorist black list by the government.

test tone generator: generates tones heard in hearing test. Waves: sine, square, sawtooth, triangle.

Targeted Family: an intimation tactic used by organized crime and the government targeting a loved one.

threat intelligence: a term for cyber security contractors that help the FBI monitor people on social media, the dark web.

thyroid: regulates hormones; affected by outside sources like radiation.

Tinfoil room: an alleged room at the Trump International Hotel that was touted safe from electronic surveillance.

Tinfoil hat: ridicule by normative thinkers in society toward believers in aliens, pseudo-science, quackery.

tinnitus: ear ringing sensation.

tort (legal): a civil wrong. i.e. negligence, battery, etc. resulting in injury.

torture psychologist: American psychologist who helped design enhanced integration techniques for black sites. E.g. Bruce Jessen and James Mitchell.

tortured souls: people with deep emotional wounds in a sad state.

tradecraft or surveillance trade craft: a term mostly used to describe spying, espionage terms like signal intelligence, HUMINT used by the Intelligence Community (IC), DoD.

traitor: a person who betrays their country in favor of another.

transient lacrimation: flowing of tears by chemical irritant. Iie. cutting onions, tear gas.

transponder: has an RFID chip inside to passively identify a tagged object. E.g. animal RFID tags.

troll: a person on the internet that is provocative for kicks.

troll factory: a term used to describe hackers planting false stories on social media in an act of hybrid warfare.

Truthers: conspiracy theories who believe 9-11 was an inside job.

tyrant: cruel oppressive rule - sometimes disguised as patriotism, counterterrorism, national security.

UAP: a new term by the government to replace UFO (unidentified flying object) so the subject matter can be politicized and taken more seriously.

Ufologist: popular personalities in the UFO community subculture who write books and give lectures at UFO conventions.

Ufology: The study of UFOs that is considered pseudo-scientific by some into the scientific method.

UFO: unidentified flying object was a 20th Century term by the Air Force to replace flying saucers since all craft reported were not saucer shaped or lenticular-shaped craft.

UFO cults: also UFO religions, cults that derived out of the Contactee Era and UFO beliefs. Giant Rock, Heaven's Gate; Raleans etc.

UFO effects: from EM interference to UFO related injuries like burns.

UFO healing: some people who claimed to be abducted by aliens claim that a physical ailment or illness was cured or gained extra knowledge and or abilities.

UFO intrusions: where UFOs appeared at sensitive sites like centers of atomic production, nuclear weapon silos, nuclear powerplants.

UFO probe: small object that comes out of a UFO, often described as a metallic sphere or Obol (ball of light).

UFO occupants: usually humanoid beings in a variety of appearance like a tight fitting coverall, helmet that come out of a UFO like a close encounter.

UFO shape: common shapes reported in the 20th century are flying saucer, egg-shape, cigar-shape, cone-shaped, sphere, and later large boomerang, back triangles.

use of force: a controversial term pertaining to law enforcement describing the amount of force used to subdue a suspect.

ultrasonic: sound waves above the upper limit of human hearing.

ultrasonic jammers: causes microphones to malfunction using USW.

ultrasonic transducers: convert alternating current (AC) into ultrasound.

useful idiot: a cheerleader for the other side although not respected by the enemy.

Vexsome Filer List: individuals or organizations frequently requesting info from the FBI who are seen as burdensome.

Voice-To-Skull (V2K): where voices were to projected inside a person's head without sound using the microwave auditory effect (MAE) or Frey effect. I.e. The Voice of God weapon; MEDUSA.

VTOL: aircraft that can take off and land vertically and can include a variety types of aircraft and helicopters.

War monger: people into blood money. Profiting from building weapons, endless war campaigns.

War on drugs: a failed war to eradicate illegal drugs during the Reagan era.

war on terrorism: post-9-11-01 doctrine to wage a war on what the government considers terrorist activity both foreign and domestic.

warrantless wireless surveillance: Edward Snowden revealed the government was lying about its surveillance capabilities. I.e. PRISM; Basket Ball; Total Information Awareness (TIA).

watch-list: a list by homeland security to keep track of subverts, radicals, potential domestic terrorist or allegedly targeted individuals.

wave-shaper: a component part of a RF weapon. A TI claimed there was an impression of a wave shaper left on a frosty window.

weasel words: words that are intentionally ambiguous or misleading like professional jargon used by PIAs or euphemisms created by the government.

weaponized government: a term referring to recent political trends where the DoJ or local-state government goes after political foes using the judicial system.

welfare-industrial complex: private corporations taking over social services functions.

welt: a red, swollen mark on the body.

What's the Frequency, Kenneth?: song by R.E.M. where two then-unknown assailants attacked journalist Dan Rather while repeating "Kenneth, what is the frequency?"

white torture: a term used to describe no-touch torture.

Willy Ley: German-American science writer and UFO skeptic.

X-rays: part of the EMF spectrum considered ionizing radiation and harmful. Often used by dentist or doctors to see bones. The NYPD had an X-ray van that could see through walls.

XKeyscore: NSA software that records the internet history of all Americans.

zero-click attacks: spyware installed on phone without person opening attachment taking advantage of zero day vulnerabilities. I.e. NSO Group

zero day vulnerabilities: flaws in an OS that the mobile phone company does not know how to fix or not able to.

Check out other books by Stephen Watson:

Covert Harassment Not Just 5G; Gene Watson - Flying Saucers (2014); Directed Energy Attacks in Los Angeles - A Memoir Of Electronic Harassment by the Authorities.

Resources:

My DE Daily Targeting Log from 2020 plus Photos:

https://stephenwatsoon.wordpress.com/248-2/

My Targeting Evidence Page:

https://stephenwatsoon.wordpress.com/my-targeting-evidence-page/

Old UFO Research Web Site archived from the 2000s.

https://www.oocities.org/topsecretresearch/

UFO Research Summary on my Wordpress Page

https://stephenwatsoon.wordpress.com/research-projects-1/

Research on targeted individuals, directed energy, private intelligence contractors, active denial, and UFOs .

https://stephenwatsoon.wordpress.com/ufo-research-archive/

Internet Archive:

https://archive.org/details/@stephen_watson